"*Faith Foundations* by Bri‸ ministry leader, parent, and grandparent. It makes core Christian truths accessible and practical for families, helping them grow in their understanding of theology and live out their faith daily. I wish I would have had this book years ago—it would have been a game-changer for my own family discipleship!"

Ryan Frank, CEO and publisher at KidzMatter

"Brian Dembowczyk is a wonderful person and communicator. I appreciate Brian's ability to articulate a clear and relevant message to leaders and parents. Whatever he is communicating, I sit up and take notice. He is authentic in his perspective and holds a solid biblical foundation. I highly recommend Brian as a speaker, as an author, and as a compassionate human. This resource by Brian is going to help parents do their most important job. Great job, Brian."

Josh Denhart, founder of Lead Ministry and KidMin Science

"A biblical understanding of children demands that we take their faith formation seriously, and Brian Dembowcyk does just that in his new resource *Faith Foundations*. Brian starts with the assumption that children are capable of understanding and responding to big theological truths about God and his work in the world and then provides tools to help families systematically explore some of these big truths together. These easy-to-use family devotions will help families learn, wonder, pray, and discuss together as they build a strong foundation of faith that will last a lifetime."

Esther Zimmerman, program chair of undergraduate ministry studies at Lancaster Bible College

"This book is the perfect resource for parents who are eager to disciple their children. Offering practical and easy-to-use activities, it makes exploring theology meaningful for the entire family. With a comprehensive overview of the key theological truths, this book helps deepen your understanding of the faith. Whether you are new to theology or looking for a stronger resource, this book equips families to grow together spiritually and explore theology in accessible, impactful ways. It is a valuable resource for fostering faith in your home and helping you disciple your children effectively."

Mimi L. Larson, executive director of the Center for Faith and Children at Trinity Evangelical Divinity School

"Brian Dembowczyk combines theological acumen along with creative and purposeful structuring to provide easy access to complex yet important theological concepts and doctrines. This much-needed work provides an engaging experience for both parent and child that enriches the whole family with a stronger understanding of God, ourselves, and the world around us in a meaningful way. *Faith Foundations* is a wonderful and welcome addition to our family discussions around the dinner table."

Daniel E. Kim, associate professor of Old Testament and Semitics at Biola University

"Parents will find *Faith Foundations* both accessible and extremely practical, filled with thoughtful questions, meaningful discussions, and Scripture-centered lessons that make faith come alive for children from preschool to middle school. Whether you are new to family devotions or looking to deepen your existing practices, this book is an invaluable resource for fostering a Christ-centered home. I highly recommend it to any family eager to pass on the faith with joy and confidence!"

Jennifer Ripley, Hughes Endowed Chair of Integration and psychology professor at Regent University

FAITH FOUNDATIONS

99 DEVOTIONS TO HELP YOUR FAMILY KNOW, LOVE & ACT LIKE JESUS

BRIAN DEMBOWCZYK

An imprint of InterVarsity Press
Downers Grove, Illinois

InterVarsity Press
P.O. Box 1400 | Downers Grove, IL 60515-1426
ivpress.com | email@ivpress.com

©2025 by Brian Dembowczyk

All rights reserved. No part of this book may be reproduced in any form without written permission from InterVarsity Press.

InterVarsity Press® is the publishing division of InterVarsity Christian Fellowship/USA®. For more information, visit intervarsity.org.

Scripture quotations, unless otherwise noted, are from the NET Bible® copyright ©1996, 2019 by Biblical Studies Press, LLC. http://netbible.com. Used by permission. All rights reserved.

Published in association with the literary agency of WTA Media LLC, Franklin, Tennessee.

While any stories in this book are true, some names and identifying information may have been changed to protect the privacy of individuals.

The publisher cannot verify the accuracy or functionality of website URLs used in this book beyond the date of publication.

Cover design: Faceout Studio, Tim Green
Interior design: Jeanna Wiggins
Cover images: © CSA Images / Vetta via Getty Images, © jumpingsack and © Dedraw Studio via Shutterstock
Interior images: © Komthong Wongsangiam / iStock via Getty Images (texture background)

ISBN 978-1-5140-1264-2 (print) | ISBN 978-1-5140-1265-9 (digital)

Printed in the United States of America ∞

Library of Congress Cataloging-in-Publication Data
Names: Dembowczyk, Brian author
Title: Faith foundations : 99 devotions to help your family know, love, and act like Jesus / Brian Dembowczyk.
Description: Downers Grove, IL : InterVarsity Press, [2025] | Includes bibliographical references and index.
Identifiers: LCCN 2025010074 (print) | LCCN 2025010075 (ebook) | ISBN 9781514012642 paperback | ISBN 9781514012659 ebook
Subjects: LCSH: Families–Religious aspects–Christianity | Families–Religious life | Devotional exercises
Classification: LCC BT707.7 .D453 2025 (print) | LCC BT707.7 (ebook)
LC record available at https://lccn.loc.gov/2025010074
LC ebook record available at https://lccn.loc.gov/2025010075

To my parents,
Edward and Cynthia Dembowczyk,

and my wife Tara's parents,
Thurman and Glenda Evans.

Your love for Tara and me

and your grandchildren, Joshua, Hannah, and Caleb,

and the example that you have lived before us and a watching world

mean more to us than you can ever know

and more than we can ever articulate.

Psalm 78:3-4

CONTENTS

How to Use Faith Foundations — 1

PART 1: God (Devotions 1-16) — 6

PART 2: Jesus (Devotions 17-25) — 40

PART 3: The Holy Spirit (Devotions 26-33) — 60

PART 4: People and Sin (Devotions 34-45) — 78

PART 5: Salvation (Devotions 46-61) — 104

PART 6: The Bible (Devotions 62-69) — 138

PART 7: Christian Living (Devotions 70-86) — 156

PART 8: The Church and Last Things (Devotions 87-99) — 192

Appendix A: Leading Your Child to Faith in Jesus — 220

Appendix B: Tips for Memorizing The Family Catechism — 225

Appendix C: Ways to Pray as a Family — 228

Notes — 231

HOW TO USE FAITH FOUNDATIONS

WORK BEGAN ON THE BELL TOWER, the final structure of a cathedral complex in Tuscany, in 1173. This eight-story tower would stand two hundred feet tall and be made of marble. But by the time the third story was complete, a problem was apparent: the tower was leaning. The foundation couldn't support the structure.

A war in the region had forced work on the tower to pause, giving the foundation time to settle. When construction resumed, workers attempted to even the tower's height by making the short side taller. The extra weight, however, caused that side to sink even more. Placing seven bells in the tower (one of which weighed eight thousand pounds) didn't help. In time, the bells stopped ringing because their swinging destabilized the tower even more.

Today, the Leaning Tower of Pisa stands at 186 feet on one side and 183 feet on the other, leaning about four degrees. The stationary bells are "rung" by electromagnetic hammers—all because of a faulty foundation.[1]

This famous tower reminds us why we cannot forsake the establishment of a sure foundation—especially when it comes to discipling our children. One of our highest callings as parents is to help lay a strong foundation of faith in our children (Deuteronomy 6:4-9). This calling is to be accomplished primarily in the home, through the power of the Holy Spirit and with the help of the church.

I believe most Christian parents want to disciple their children, but they aren't sure how. It's important to remember that God hasn't given you this task to complete on your own. The Holy Spirit is with you! He will help you, guide you, encourage you, and strengthen you. God knows that you too are a disciple, learning and growing. That's where the partnership of the local church comes in. The church helps equip you as a parent to fulfill this calling even as it fulfills its calling to help you grow as a disciple.

Understanding that you play a significant role in laying a faith foundation in your child is one thing; understanding what that foundation is to be is another. Coming to saving faith in Jesus is a critical step, but it's not the entire foundation. Forgiveness from sin is just the first part of an amazing journey. A child who has trusted in Jesus but doesn't grow in faith misses out on a life of blessing and purpose, sometimes for years or even decades.

We want the best for our children, and the best is Jesus. Not just some of Jesus; all of Jesus. That's why it's so important to roll up our sleeves and help our children know and trust Jesus, then help them put their faith into practice by living like Jesus. That faith foundation will last.

In this book you will encounter ninety-nine devotions that work together to help you do this—to craft a strong, firm foundation of faith for your child. Some devotions will cover the basics of the faith, or as Paul put it, the spiritual "milk" (1 Corinthians 3:2). Others will address some of the deeper truths, or the "solid food." But they are all designed to be accessible and meaningful for you and your family. The thread that runs through all these devotions, holding them together, is something called The Family Catechism.

THE FAMILY CATECHISM

A catechism is a series of questions and answers that concern the basics of the faith and are meant to be recited and memorized.[2] Catechisms may not be well-known in some circles, but they have been used in the church since at least the sixteenth-century Protestant Reformation. Martin Luther wrote the 374-question Small Catechism (*Der Kleine Katechismus*) in 1529. That was followed by the 373-question Geneva Catechism by John Calvin in 1542, the 129-question Heidelberg Catechism in 1563, the 107-question Westminster Shorter Catechism in 1646, and the 114-question Baptist Catechism in 1677. Several of these, such as Luther's and Calvin's, were intended to be used primarily by families.[3]

The *Faith Foundations* catechism was developed with your family in mind, and it will guide you on a natural progression through the Bible's big truths (called *theology*). The catechism's topics and vocabulary are intended to be approachable for your family but also stretch you at times. In this way they will help you enjoy milk and meat.

The devotions are divided into eight sections based on the eight parts of The Family Catechism: questions about (1) God, (2) Jesus, (3) the Holy Spirit, (4) people and sin, (5) salvation, (6) the Bible, (7) Christian living, and (8) the church and last things. But keep in mind that the big truths of the Bible are often interconnected. Take the first category, "Questions about God," for example. It isn't possible to explore truths about God without mentioning Jesus and the Holy Spirit. It's also not possible to talk about Jesus without rubbing shoulders with some of the ideas of people, sin, and salvation. Lean into this overlap; it can show your child the interconnectedness of God's truth.

The Family Catechism questions build on each other, with one question setting up the next. This means it's ideal to walk through the devotions in order, although that isn't necessary. Each question can stand alone, but some are helped by the context provided by an earlier question.

LEADING A FAMILY DEVOTION

When you choose a time for family devotions, look at your weekly schedule and decide what will be easiest to maintain consistency. Dinner often works well.

How long should your devotions last? If you're just starting out or have young children, it might be five minutes as you eat dessert. Ten or fifteen minutes is the sweet spot for many families. Twenty minutes, perhaps spanning the full meal, would likely begin pushing the upper boundary. Regardless of how you start, know that your practice will likely change with the season of life you're in, and it may even change week to week. Sometimes you might only squeeze in a couple of minutes, and that's okay!

In terms of frequency, once a week is an ideal starting point. Less frequent than that makes it hard to develop a rhythm. More often could be too much. Ultimately, you can determine what works best for your family. Each devotion follows the same seven steps.

1. Read The Family Catechism question and answer. Begin by reading the catechism question and answer, then review it a few times. If you are memorizing, use the tips provided in appendix B. For the second devotion and beyond, spend some time reviewing prior catechism questions.

2. Read the Scripture. Read or invite your child to read the Bible passage aloud. For families with young children, a shorter reading suggestion is provided in parentheses.

3. Read the devotion. You can read the devotion word for word aloud, or you can paraphrase it for your family. If you have older children, invite them to read the devotions aloud at times.

4. Engage in the discussion questions. Each devotion includes four discussion questions. At this point you can pray that your family will go "off script" as you explore what's on your child's mind and heart.

The first question is designed to "prime the pump" for conversation, with no right or wrong answer, and often focuses on something fun. The second question is always answered on a scale of one to ten. This is designed to create room for natural follow-up questions. If, for example, your child scores herself with a seven in terms of how much God loves her (with ten being perfectly), you can ask her why she thinks God doesn't love her more than she indicated.

The third question is meant to prompt more questions, something we want to embrace in discipleship. Do your best to create a safe space where all questions are welcome, including yours. The goal isn't to answer the questions but to train our families that asking questions is good. Questions require humility and show we're engaged with God's Word. Consider using a notebook to record the questions asked and any answers you discover.

The fourth question is meant to invite curiosity. Encourage everyone (including yourself) to make "wonder statements." These are expressions of curiosity and awe that get us "underneath" the Bible, helping us remember that we're interacting with true, historical stories. A wonder statement concerning Israel's crossing of the Red Sea (Exodus 14) might be, "I wonder if the Israelites saw fish in the walls of water." There's no answer to this statement, but it shows deeper thinking. Wonder statements can help foster worship and at times they can simply be fun!

5. Share the Jesus Connection. The Jesus Connection is designed to guide every devotion to Jesus. Each Jesus Connection concludes with an application question, inviting you to consider how you will live more like Jesus. Encourage answers that are practical. This might also be a good time to review the previous devotion's Jesus Connection to see how everyone lived it out. Celebrate even the smallest win. Give grace and encouragement to any failures. Make this a time of mutual encouragement, grace, and love.

6. Pray. Wrap up with a time of prayer. A simple, one-sentence prayer is provided. Beyond that, feel free to develop your approach to prayer time or rotate through different ways to pray, such as those provided in appendix C.

7. Plan a family activity. The family activity is designed to help move truths off the page and into real life through times of playing, exploring, blessing, experimenting, competing, creating, observing, serving, visiting, gathering, and worshiping. At times you might engage in the family activity as part of your family devotion, but most often it will be a separate time.

PART 1

GOD

AT FIRST GLANCE, defining God can seem like we're trying to define blue. God is just God, right? That's true to a point. Even God has defined himself this way. In the Old Testament, one of the most common Hebrew names for God is *Yahweh*, which is often translated as "Lord" (with small capital letters, to make it stand out from "Lord," which translates as something else). *Yahweh* basically means "I am" or "I exist" (see Exodus 3:14). So, when Moses asked God this very question—who are you?—God's response was simply, "I am God." But God didn't define himself only in this way in the Bible. He also gave us many other names (e.g., Elohim, Adonai, El Shaddai) and characteristics (e.g., loving, faithful, just) to know him by.

How, then, do we begin to define God for our kids? Do we take the way that seems overly simple or the way that seems overly complex? Perhaps the best approach is in the middle: focusing on an overarching description that is unique to God—a description that provides glimpses of his other important characteristics but that is simple enough for our kids to get their arms around. A description like this: "God is the creator and ruler of all things." This is basically how God chose to introduce himself to us in Genesis 1. It's simple enough, but it hints at several important undergirding truths. God is immensely powerful; he must be to make everything by speaking. He is unique; he alone isn't created. He has all authority; that means he makes the rules for how everything works, including us. And he loves us and wants to know us; that's the very reason we exist.

The first section of *Faith Foundations* focuses on what you'd likely expect—who God is, a subject known as "theology proper" (theology means "the study of God"). Your family will have the opportunity to interact with sixteen questions about God, covering some ideas that are fairly easy and others that can be challenging. As you guide conversations about our amazing God with your family, don't lose sight of the two big ideas we started with, that God is our creator and ruler. If the waters start to get too deep, retreat to these calmer waters. Also, don't miss the proper response that talking about God should prompt: gratitude, love, and worship. God is a good God. He gives us life. He provides for us. And he used his infinite power to provide forgiveness for our sins through Jesus because of his remarkable love for us.

1 WHO IS GOD?

God is our creator and he is the ruler of everything.

GENESIS 1:1-31 (OR 1:1)

God made everything. That's how we meet him in the very first verse of the Bible, so it must be important to know. God made the sun, the moon, the stars, and all the planets. He made them all and he placed them right where he wants each one to be. God made the mountains, the oceans, the trees, the plants, and the animals too. Everything we see—and everything we can't see because it's too small or too far away—was made by God. That includes you and me and all people everywhere. God made us most special of all. God is a wonderful creator!

Because God made everything, everything belongs to God. And because everything belongs to God, God is in charge of everything. That includes you and me and all people. As our ruler, God makes the rules we are to follow. Sometimes we don't like to follow rules, but all God's rules are good because he is good. God loves us and wants what's best for us. He wants us to do what pleases him and what's good for us. He wants us not to do what doesn't please him and what's not good for us. When we follow God's rules, he's happy and so are we. God is a wonderful ruler!

Never forget that God loves you. Never forget that God cares about you. Never forget that God wants what's best for you. God's rules might not always be easy to follow but that's where faith comes in. When we trust that God is always good and loving and that he always knows what's best and that he always wants what's best, *having* to obey God becomes *getting* to obey God.

▶ *What's your most favorite thing that God made?*

WHO IS GOD? 9

▶ How much do you want to follow God's rules?

I REALLY REALLY DON'T — I REALLY REALLY DO

▶ What questions do you have so far?

▶ What are you wondering about because of what you've heard?

PRAYER

God, thank you for making everything there is, and most especially, thank you for making us. Amen.

FAMILY ACTIVITY: PLAY

Do it. Play a favorite board game, but let everyone make up their own rules as you play. Then play a round with the set rules.

Discuss it. Ask which was more fun. Talk about how we might think not having rules is better, but it's not.

Connect it. Share that God's rules are always for our best.

▼ JESUS CONNECTION ▼

While Jesus was on earth, he followed all God the Father's rules: the big ones, the small ones, and the ones in between. We can't obey all God's rules like Jesus, but we can be like Jesus by wanting to obey God. As you grow to love God more, you'll likely come to obey God more. But even when you don't, never forget that your creator and ruler always loves you.

▶ What can you do to remember that God always loves you, even when you struggle to obey?

2 HOW MANY GODS ARE THERE?

There is one God who exists in three persons: God the Father, God the Son, and God the Holy Spirit.

MATTHEW 3:13-17 (OR 3:16-17)

Some things are hard to understand. How does a big, heavy plane soar through the air or a big, heavy ship float on the water? And how in the world does math work? These things are hard to understand, but they're not impossible to understand; some people can answer these questions. But there are things about God that no one can figure out. Today's question and answer is one of them.

It isn't too hard to understand that there's one God; the hard part is understanding that there's one God in three persons. God the Father, God the Son, and God the Holy Spirit aren't three different beings; there's only one God. The Father, Son, and Spirit aren't each one-third of God either, as if we must add them together to get one full God. Rather, God is one God in three persons and each person is fully God, a truth often called *the Trinity*.

You won't find the word *Trinity* in the Bible, but you can see proof of it there, like in Matthew 3. As Jesus, who is God the Son, was baptized, God the Holy Spirit came down from heaven like a dove and God the Father spoke from heaven. We see that each person is different, but they each worked together in that moment as one God.

It's okay if this is still confusing. The Trinity is one of the greatest mysteries of our faith. And in a way, we can be glad we don't understand it. God wouldn't be very impressive if we had him all figured out! As you read the Bible and meet God the Father, God the Son, and God the Holy Spirit, just remember you're meeting one God in three persons, the wonderful and sometimes mysterious God we love and obey.

▶ **What are some things you don't understand about God, the Bible, or the world?**

HOW MANY GODS ARE THERE?   11

▶ How confusing is the Trinity to you?

I'M SO LOST!   I'VE GOT IT!

▶ What questions do you have so far?

▶ What are you wondering about because of what you've heard?

PRAYER

God, thank you for being such a big, amazing God who we cannot fully understand, but thank you for giving us the Bible to help us understand you more. Amen.

FAMILY ACTIVITY: EXPLORE

Do it. Examine the inside of a computer, a car engine, or some other complicated machine. If possible, refer to a user's manual to identify the parts you see.

Discuss it. Talk about how you might not understand how that machine works, but that doesn't stop you from trusting that it does work or from using it.

Connect it. Share how our faith is a lot like that—we might not understand all of God, but we can still trust him and follow him!

▼ JESUS CONNECTION ▼

While Jesus was on earth, he acted in perfect harmony with the Father and the Holy Spirit. The Holy Spirit helped Jesus do all the Father wanted him to do. And that's how we're made to live too! Each day as we look to live like Jesus, we don't do that alone. Instead, the Holy Spirit is with us to help us. As the Holy Spirit guides you and empowers you, you'll live more like Jesus, which delights the Father.

▶ *What's something you enjoy doing that you know delights God?*

3. WHAT DOES IT MEAN THAT GOD IS A PERSON?

That God is a person means he thinks, feels, and makes choices.

PSALM 92:1-6 (OR 93:2, 5)

Think of one of your friends. You're probably picturing your friend's face in your mind and thinking, "Yup, that's my friend." That's because when we think of a person, we usually think of a physical body. So when you think of your friend, it's normal to think of the physical body that you can see. But your friend is so much more than a physical body. A big part of your friend is his or her ability to think, feel, and make choices. We can't see those things, but they are what make each of us unique; they make us who we really are.

This is why we can say that God is one God in three persons, even though God the Father and God the Spirit don't have a physical body. And although God the Son came to earth in a human body, he didn't have one before that. If this is confusing, that's okay. We'll talk more about that last part in questions seventeen, eighteen, and nineteen. But for now, just know that what makes the Father, Son, and Holy Spirit persons is that they each think, feel, and make choices.

That's what we see in Psalm 92, where God the Father does each. The Father loves (v. 2), is faithful (v. 2), and makes plans (v. 5). For him to love us, he feels love for us. For him to be faithful, he makes a choice to be faithful. For him to make plans, he thinks about what to do. This is what makes the Father a person, and in different places in the Bible, we see the same for the Son and Spirit.

▶ *What are some things you've thought, felt, or chosen this week?*

WHAT DOES IT MEAN THAT GOD IS A PERSON?

▶ How does it make you feel knowing God thinks about you, feels love for you, and makes choices concerning you?

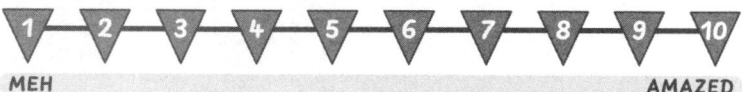

MEH — AMAZED

▶ What questions do you have so far?

▶ What are you wondering about because of what you've heard?

PRAYER

God, thank you for thinking about us, loving us, and choosing to provide Jesus for us. Amen.

FAMILY ACTIVITY: BLESS

Do it. Think about what you appreciate about your extended family, friends, neighbors, and others you know. Make a card, send a text, or call one or two of the people you think of, letting them know how grateful you are for them.

Discuss it. Talk about what makes people unique and special.

Connect it. Share that God made each of us special to remind us that he, our maker, is so special.

▼ JESUS CONNECTION ▼

We learn much about what it means to be a person from Jesus. He shows us how to think, feel, and choose in ways that are true to how God made us and that honor him. To act like Jesus is to think, feel, and choose like Jesus. We won't do that perfectly, of course, but with the Spirit's help, each day we can be more of who we were made to be.

▶ How can you include Jesus in what you think, feel, or choose this week?

4 WHAT DOES IT MEAN THAT GOD IS ETERNAL?

That God is eternal means he has always existed and he always will exist.

PSALM 90:1-6 (OR 90:1-2)

What is the biggest number you can think of? Do you have it in your mind? Okay, here's the problem: no matter how big your number is, we can add one to it and it's no longer the biggest number. And then we can add one to that new number and it's no longer the biggest number either! There's simply no biggest number. Numbers just keep going and going without end.

Now, replace numbers with days and that's what eternal means. It's time going on without end. It just keeps going and going and going forever. That's hard to imagine, but eternal is an even bigger head-scratcher than that! It doesn't just go on forever into the future; it also goes on forever into the past. Eternal means there's no ending and there's no beginning. That's even harder to imagine, isn't it?

When we trust in Jesus, we're promised an eternal future with him (John 10:28). That means all believers of all time will be with Jesus and have the perfect life God intended and experience only good things forever and ever. But we still had a beginning. And so did the mountains, oceans, stars, and planets. Nothing existed until God made it. Everything has a beginning—except God.

God alone has no ending and no beginning. He will be around forever and he has been around forever. That's what we mean when we say that God is eternal. And that's what Moses marveled at when he wrote Psalm 90. God is older than all the generations of people (v. 1). He's older than the mountains and older than the world (v. 2). He's always been and always will be. He's forever forward and he's forever backward. Only him!

▶ Which is harder to imagine: forever in the future or forever in the past? Why?

WHAT DOES IT MEAN THAT GOD IS ETERNAL?

▶ How excited are you to live with Jesus forever?

YAWN!   WOW!

▶ What questions do you have so far?

▶ What are you wondering about because of what you've heard?

PRAYER

God, thank you for promising us a wonderful, amazing forever with you when we trust in Jesus. Amen.

FAMILY ACTIVITY: EXPLORE

Do it. Visit a cemetery and try to find the person who was born earliest, the person who died earliest, and the person who lived the longest, or interview your neighbors or church family to see who was born earliest.

Discuss it. Talk about how God makes each person for a reason and gives us each the gift of life.

Connect it. Share that when we trust in Jesus, life on earth isn't the end. God has promised us a wonderful forever with Jesus.

▼ JESUS CONNECTION ▼

Knowing we will live forever with Jesus doesn't mean our time now doesn't matter. It matters because it's the only time when we can help others know and trust in Jesus so they too will live forever with him. Jesus was on earth only for about thirty-three years, but he used that time to the max. To live like Jesus means trying to make the most of our time by helping others come to know him.

▶ How can you use some time this week to help others know Jesus?

5 WHAT DOES IT MEAN THAT GOD IS SPIRIT?

That God is spirit means he does not have a physical body.

JOHN 4:19-24 (OR 4:24)

In John 4, the woman talking with Jesus was a Samaritan. Jesus was a Jew. The Samaritan people and Jewish people were distant relatives, but they didn't get along very well. Even though they had once been one people, in Jesus' day they avoided each other. That's why the Samaritans worshiped God in their own land instead of going to Jerusalem. Was that wrong of them?

From the days of Moses up to the days of Solomon, God's people were supposed to worship him at the tabernacle, a portable tent. But then Solomon built the temple in Jerusalem. This was a permanent building and became the place where people were to worship God. But Jesus told the Samaritan woman that things were about to change again. Because of who Jesus is and what he would do in giving up his life, worship would change. It wouldn't matter where people worshiped anymore because God is spirit.

We live in a physical world. We focus on what we can see, hear, touch, smell, and taste. But there's a spiritual world all around us too. We can't see, hear, touch, smell, or taste it, but it's just as real. This spiritual world is where God the Father and God the Spirit live without a physical body. Jesus is a little different. He started without a physical body, but he came to earth in one. Jesus became human so he could die and pay the punishment for sin, then rise again. Now when someone trusts in Jesus, the Holy Spirit comes to live within them. That's why God can be worshiped anywhere, just like Jesus promised! God is always with us!

▶ *Which of the five senses would you least want to do without?*

WHAT DOES IT MEAN THAT GOD IS SPIRIT? 17

▶ How does an unseen spiritual world all around you make you feel?

SORT OF SCARED — SORT OF EXCITED

▶ What questions do you have so far?

▶ What are you wondering about because of what you've heard?

PRAYER

God, thank you that we can worship you anywhere at any time because of what Jesus has done for us. Amen.

FAMILY ACTIVITY: EXPERIMENT

Do it. Research gravity experiments online and choose a few to do as a family.

Discuss it. Talk about how gravity is real and all around us even if we can't see it, hear it, touch it, smell it, or taste it.

Connect it. Share that the spiritual world is like gravity. Just because we can't see it doesn't mean it's not real.

▼ JESUS CONNECTION ▼

Just because God is spirit doesn't mean the physical world isn't important. Look at what Jesus did while he was here on earth. He taught people truth, but he also fed them and healed them. To live like Jesus is to do the same. It's surely important to tell others about how they can trust in Jesus to be forgiven, but it's also important to meet their physical needs when we can.

▶ How can you help meet a physical need of someone around you this week?

6

WHAT DOES IT MEAN THAT GOD IS HOLY?

That God is holy means he is pure and set apart from sin.

ISAIAH 6:1-7 (OR 6:3)

Have you ever made chocolate milk? It's pretty easy. All you need to do is put some chocolate powder or chocolate syrup into milk and stir. The chocolate mixes all throughout the milk and it becomes chocolate milk. But have you ever tried to make white milk from chocolate milk? You can't really do that. Once the chocolate is in the milk, there's no way to get it back out.

That's like what sin has done to the world. It's gotten into everyone and everything. Except God. Sin hasn't gotten into him at all. It hasn't even touched him. That's because God is holy, or set apart from sin. Put another way, God is pure. This is what we read about in Isaiah 6. There, Isaiah the prophet had a vision of God in heaven. He saw God sitting on a high throne and majestic angelic creatures surrounding him calling out, "Holy, holy, holy."

It's an amazing scene, right? But surprisingly, Isaiah wasn't excited to see God. That's because Isaiah knew he was full of sin and God is holy. And that means Isaiah shouldn't have been near such a holy God. Because God is holy, he cannot simply turn a blind eye to sin. All sin—from the biggest, worst sins to the smallest, plainest sins—must be dealt with. It must be removed from us if we want to be friends with God. But just like we can't turn chocolate milk back into white milk, there's no way we can undo what sin has done. But thankfully, our amazing God made a way for that to happen through Jesus!

▶ Why do you think the creatures said "holy" three times?

WHAT DOES IT MEAN THAT GOD IS HOLY? 19

▶ How holy do you think you are?

I'M ABSOLUTELY FILTHY I'M SPARKLING CLEAN

▶ What questions do you have so far?

▶ What are you wondering about because of what you've heard?

PRAYER

God, thank you that you are holy and that you made the one and only way for us to be holy through Jesus. Amen.

FAMILY ACTIVITY: COMPETE

Do it. Pour several different kinds of breakfast cereals into a pile. Take turns separating the cereals to see who can do it the fastest.

Discuss it. As you enjoy a bowl of (clean!) cereal, talk about the challenges of separating the cereal, especially its tiny pieces or powder. Point out that it's almost impossible to separate the cereal perfectly.

Connect it. Share how this is a picture of holiness and how we need God's help to keep us separate from sin.

▼ JESUS CONNECTION ▼

Jesus is holy, but that didn't stop him from stepping into the world and being around sinful people who needed him. In the same way, we aren't supposed to hide in a "holy huddle" to avoid sin. Instead, as the old saying goes, we're to be in the world but not of the world. Jesus showed us the perfect example of living a holy life among sinful, hurting people. To live like him means we do the same.

▶ What are some ways you can be around sinful people without sinning?

7 WHAT DOES IT MEAN THAT GOD IS LOVE?

That God is love means he faithfully and perfectly cares for people and he is the source and the standard of love.

1 JOHN 4:8

We use the word *love* quite often, don't we? One minute, we might say, "I love you" to a family member. Then, we might turn around and say that we love ice cream. Or that we'd love to go see a movie. We use the same word, but it doesn't mean quite the same thing each time. In fact, *love* is used so much and in so many ways that some people don't know what it really means. But the question isn't a matter of what love is. It's about *who* love is. That might sound funny, but it's the key to understanding, and then experiencing, love. Love isn't a thing; love is a person. God is love.

That's what 1 John 4:8 tells us. God doesn't just love us and the world he made, although he certainly does that. And God doesn't just act in loving ways, although, again, he certainly does that too. It's much more than that. God *is* love. It's part of his basic nature. Love is part of who he is. That's why God always acts in love. He can't not act in love because that would go against who he is. And whenever God acts in love—which is all the time—he does so perfectly. He perfectly and completely lovingly cares for you!

As if that's not amazing enough, God isn't just love and he doesn't just act in love all the time; he is the source of love. When we trust in Jesus, we're made new and God fills us with his love so we can love others. So if you want to know what love is or how to love, all you need to do is look to our amazing loving God.

▶ **What are ten things that you love?**

WHAT DOES IT MEAN THAT GOD IS LOVE?

▶ How sure are you that God loves you?

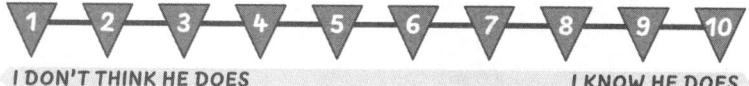

I DON'T THINK HE DOES I KNOW HE DOES

▶ What questions do you have so far?

▶ What are you wondering about because of what you've heard?

PRAYER

God, thank you for loving us completely and always, no matter what. Amen.

FAMILY ACTIVITY: EXPLORE

Do it. Visit a hardware store and examine different measuring devices. Afterward, stop for ice cream, doughnuts, or some other treat.

Discuss it. As you eat, talk about how the restaurant building wouldn't be standing without accurate measurements and what you're eating likely needs precise measurements too (e.g., ingredients, temperature, time).

Connect it. Share that for love to work best, it needs the right standard. We don't love based on how the world defines it; we love based on God's love!

▼ JESUS CONNECTION ▼

It's not hard to see how much Jesus loved people while he was on earth. He cared for people—deeply and fully—even when they were difficult to love or unloved by others. He even loved people who didn't love him back. Loving lovable people is kind of easy. But to live like Jesus means we go beyond that and love unlovable people too.

▶ What one thing can you do this week to begin loving someone new?

8. WHAT DOES IT MEAN THAT GOD IS JUST?

That God is just means he is perfectly consistent, fair, and right in all he does, and he is the source and the standard of justice.

MICAH 6:7-8 (OR 6:8)

When we use the word *just*, we usually mean only. "I just want ice cream," means "I only want ice cream." But *just* can mean something different too. It can mean to be fair or to be marked by justice. That's what we mean when we say God is just. God is always fair in everything he does. And he doesn't only act in justice; he defines it. When we are just, it's because we are acting like God and following his ways.

This is what we see in Micah 6. Often in the Old Testament, God's people thought that all God wanted from them was proper worship. As long as they went to the right place of worship, offered the right sacrifices, and prayed the right prayers, God was pleased. But what they didn't understand was that the way they lived was to be an act of worship too. And God wasn't pleased with how they were living. They were mistreating one another. The rich and powerful were getting away with wrongdoing. So God told them their acts of worship meant nothing if they didn't live with justice, faithfulness, and obedience.

We see here and in many other places in the Bible that God's heart is for those in need. He cares deeply for those who are being wronged, those who are forgotten, and those who feel they are without hope. God loves these people and he wants justice for them. He wants wrongs to be punished and he wants fairness and righteousness for everyone. And he wants us to be part of that. God's justice is for us, and he wants us to partner with him and stand for justice for others as best as we can.

▶ How does it feel when you are treated unfairly?

WHAT DOES IT MEAN THAT GOD IS JUST? 23

▶ How do you feel when you see someone else being mistreated?

GLAD IT ISN'T ME   AS UPSET AS IF IT WERE ME

▶ What questions do you have so far?

▶ What are you wondering about because of what you've heard?

PRAYER

God, thank you for always being fair to us and for wanting everyone to experience justice. Amen.

FAMILY ACTIVITY: CREATE

Do it. Search online for strange laws. Take turns to see who can make up the strangest or funniest laws for your family.

Discuss it. Talk about how governments can make up some odd laws and that they aren't always fair or just. That's because governments are made of people and people aren't perfect.

Connect it. Share how some of God's laws might be difficult for us to understand, but they are all good and just.

▼ JESUS CONNECTION ▼

Part of being just is being fair to everyone. That's how Jesus was when he was on earth. Jesus didn't play favorites. He didn't treat people with money, or anyone else, better than others. Instead, Jesus spent time with the rich and powerful and the poor and powerless. As we try to live like Jesus, we can do the same and treat everyone with fairness.

▶ How can you treat others the same way you treat your favorite friends?

9 WHAT DOES IT MEAN THAT GOD IS OMNIPRESENT?

That God is omnipresent means he is present everywhere at once.

PSALM 139:7-10 (OR 139:7-8)

As people, we can be in only one place at a time. Sometimes we wish that weren't true, but it is. That's not true of God, though. He's omnipresent. *Omni* means "all," so this is like saying that God is "all present." Or, more simply, that he's everywhere at once.

This amazing truth was on David's mind when he wrote Psalm 139. There's no place a person can go without God being there. God is present in the highest of heavens and he's present in the lowest parts of the earth. He's at the farthest point east and he's at the farthest point west. There isn't a square inch of the entire universe that is absent of God.

Now this doesn't mean God is so big he takes up every inch of space in the universe. God is spirit; he has no body to take up all that space. Also, if that were true, then only part of God would be in one place at a time. There would be one part of God here, another part of him over there, and a different part of him way, way over there. But that's not how it is. God is fully present everywhere at the same time. God is fully here, there, and way, way over there too.

So what does this mean for us? Something wonderful! It means we're never alone. We're never forgotten or neglected. Our loving, powerful, watchful God is always with us, and he's always with us fully. That's a wonderfully comforting thought, isn't it?

▶ *Where is one place you'd love to be able to go?*

WHAT DOES IT MEAN THAT GOD IS OMNIPRESENT?

▶ How does it make you feel knowing God is always with you?

A LITTLE PRIVACY PLEASE! THAT'S FANTASTIC!

▶ What questions do you have so far?

▶ What are you wondering about because of what you've heard?

PRAYER

God, thank you for always being with us and never leaving us, no matter what. Amen.

FAMILY ACTIVITY: EXPLORE

Do it. Pick a country that is far away from where you live. Research the languages people speak there, its culture, art, clothing, and so forth. If possible, find recipes from that country and make a meal.

Discuss it. As you eat, talk about what it might be like to live in that country and if anyone would like to do that.

Connect it. Share how God is present in the country you researched and that he loves every person who lives there.

▼ JESUS CONNECTION ▼

While Jesus was on earth, he made it a priority to spend time with the Father. He'd often go off by himself and pray. As we grow to live more like Jesus, this is one of the best things we can do too. God is always with us, so he's always there for us, welcoming us to talk with him, worship him, and spend time with him.

▶ When will you spend time with God today and what will you do?

10

WHAT DOES IT MEAN THAT GOD IS OMNISCIENT?

That God is omniscient means he knows everything that was, that is, that will be, and that could be.

MATTHEW 10:26-31 (OR 10:29-31)

The Major League Baseball season is long. It usually begins in late March and runs into November, with each team playing at least 162 games. During the 2023 season, batters came to the plate 184,478 times and saw a total of 718,247 pitches.[1] That's a lot! Now, could you imagine taking a test where you had to write down each batter's name, how many pitches he faced, what each pitch was, and the result of each pitch? Impossible, right? There's no way a person could know all that. How about doing that for every season since baseball began in 1869? That would be an absurd test!

But God knows all of that and so much more. He knows the temperature for each game, how many people were in the stands, what their names were, what they snacked on, and who caught foul balls. The reason is because God is omniscient—meaning he's all-knowing. And God isn't just all-knowing about baseball. He knows everything about everything. That's what we see in Matthew 10. He knows where every bird is right now, and he knows how many hairs are on each person's head (the average is between 90,000 to 150,000 hairs).[2]

If that doesn't impress you enough, God knows even more than that. He knows everything that will be and even what could have been. Think about all the choices you made today. God knows what would have happened if you'd made a different choice each time. This same God who knows everything about everything knows you and he loves you completely.

▶ What would you want to know everything about?

WHAT DOES IT MEAN THAT GOD IS OMNISCIENT?

▶ How does God knowing everything about you make you feel?

IT BOTHERS ME — IT COMFORTS ME

▶ What questions do you have so far?

▶ What are you wondering about because of what you've heard?

PRAYER

God, thank you for knowing everything so we can fully trust you. Amen.

FAMILY ACTIVITY: PLAY

Do it. Play a trivia game like Trivial Pursuit or Trivial Pursuit Junior.

Discuss it. After the game, talk about how much there is to know in the world and how little any of us really knows.

Connect it. Share about how God knows everything and marvel in that truth.

▼ JESUS CONNECTION ▼

Jesus talked about the Father knowing all about birds and the number of hairs on our heads to comfort people. Nothing happens without him knowing. Jesus didn't just care that people trusted in him for salvation; he also cared about their mental, emotional, and physical well-being. As we look for ways to live like Jesus, one way we can do that is by caring about people the same way.

▶ This week, who can you give a note to or share a kind word with to show you care about them?

11

WHAT DOES IT MEAN THAT GOD IS OMNIPOTENT?

That God is omnipotent means he can do anything that is according to his character and will.

GENESIS 18:9-14 (OR 18:14)

Older people usually don't have children. But when God promised to give Abraham and Sarah a son, they were quite old: Abraham was seventy-five years old and Sarah was sixty-five. Nearly twenty-five years after God made that promise, they still didn't have a child, and the chances of them having a child weren't getting any better. In fact, they were getting much, much worse. That's probably why Sarah laughed when she heard a visitor tell Abraham that she'd have a baby within a year. In response, the visitor told Sarah something very important: nothing is impossible for God. That's because God is all-powerful, which is also called being *omnipotent*.

Sometimes people explain how God is omnipotent by saying he can do anything. But that's not quite true. Actually, God can't do anything. That might sound shocking, but it's true. For one thing, God can't do anything that goes against his character. God can't stop being God. He can't stop being loving, or just, or all-knowing. For another thing, God can't do anything that goes against his will or what he has promised. So, for example, God can't destroy the world by a flood again because he promised Noah he wouldn't do that (Genesis 9:11). Is God powerful enough to do that? For sure! But can he do that? No, he can't, because he said he wouldn't.

Other than those things, though, God can indeed do anything. There's nothing that limits his power to do what he pleases. This is what the Bible's miracles teach us. Our God is powerful enough to give children to an elderly couple, part seas, stop the sun, calm storms, heal the sick, and even raise the dead—all because he loves people and to bring about his wonderful and perfect plans.

▶ *If you had the power to do anything, what would it be?*

WHAT DOES IT MEAN THAT GOD IS OMNIPOTENT?

▶ How much do you believe that God can do anything that you need?

1 — 2 — 3 — 4 — 5 — 6 — 7 — 8 — 9 — 10
HE'S POWERLESS — HE'S ALL-POWERFUL

▶ What questions do you have so far?

▶ What are you wondering about because of what you've heard?

PRAYER

God, thank you for being all-powerful and always providing for us and protecting us. Amen.

FAMILY ACTIVITY: CREATE

Do it. Draw yourselves as superheroes. What would your costume look like? What powers would you have? Would you have any weaknesses?

Discuss it. Talk about how superheroes are a lot of fun, but they're all make-believe.

Connect it. Share that unlike superheroes, God is real and he is all-powerful with no weaknesses.

▼ JESUS CONNECTION ▼

Jesus did many amazing miracles while he was on earth, mostly because people were in need and he felt compassion for them. When Jesus saw hungry people, he cared about them, so he fed them. When Jesus saw sick people, he loved them, so he healed them. We might not be able to do the miracles Jesus did, but we can care for people like he did and do everything in our power to help them.

▶ *How can you help someone in need this week?*

12

WHAT DOES IT MEAN THAT GOD IS INFINITE?

That God is infinite means he is limitless in all his attributes.

1 KINGS 8:27-30 (OR 8:27, 29)

We live with many limits on what we can do. We only have twenty-four hours in a day, and we have to sleep for about eight to ten of them. We need oxygen to breathe and we need the outside temperature to be in a certain range to live. We run out of energy if we don't eat. Our brains can handle only so much information. We can be in only one place at a time. Even the strongest of us can lift only so much. Even the fastest of us can run only so fast. We are finite, which means we have limits. This explains why there's so much we can't do. God, however, is infinite—he has no limits. He isn't limited by the hours in a day. He has no body needing oxygen or a certain outside temperature. He doesn't run out of energy. He's all-knowing, all-present, and all-powerful. He's limitless. Whatever God is, he is to the fullest.

This is what Solomon understood as he completed building the temple in Jerusalem. The temple would be God's dwelling place on earth but only in one way. The temple would be where God's presence would be available to his people, but not only there. God is omnipresent; he can't be limited to any one place, not even the temple.

God being infinite can help us understand all his attributes, which is another word for his characteristics, or things that are true about him. Each one is immeasurable; it's infinite. How much grace does God have? Infinite. Love? Infinite. Goodness? Infinite. And on and on and on. And here's some wonderful news: all that infinite grace and love and goodness and much more is directed right toward you!

▶ *What is the highest number you can count to?*

WHAT DOES IT MEAN THAT GOD IS INFINITE?

▶ How do your limitations make you feel?

1—2—3—4—5—6—7—8—9—10
FRUSTRATED   FINE

▶ What questions do you have so far?

▶ What are you wondering about because of what you've heard?

PRAYER

God, thank you for being limitless in your goodness and love and kindness to us. Amen.

FAMILY ACTIVITY: EXPLORE

Do it. Visit a beach or river, or a playground with a sandbox (or get some sand from a store). Pick up a handful of sand and try to count the grains. Think about how many grains of sand are on the planet. Then, if you're near water, notice the water that seems to have no end.

Discuss it. Talk about how sand and water seem limitless, but they are limited.

Connect it. Share that unlike sand and water, God truly is limitless.

▼ JESUS CONNECTION ▼

Jesus is the limitless Son of God. And yet for a time he chose to limit himself when he came to earth and became a human too. It took great humility for Jesus to do this. As we look for ways to live like Jesus, we can't copy his limitless nature, but we can copy his humility. In humility, we can focus more on God and others than ourselves.

▶ How can you humbly use your limited resources of time, energy, money, and so forth for God and others this week?

13. WHAT DOES IT MEAN THAT GOD IS IMMUTABLE?

That God is immutable means he does not change in who he is, what he wills, or what he has promised.

NUMBERS 23:18-20 (OR 23:19)

They say only one thing in life stays the same: change. Sometimes we're glad things change. It's fun to get older and bigger and be able to do new things. Other times, though, we aren't very excited about change. Moving to a new town or moving up a grade in school can be sad or frightening. But whether it's good or bad, we simply can't avoid change.

Not God, though. God doesn't change at all. Never. None of his characteristics change. He is who he always has been and who he always will be. What he wills doesn't change either. What he wants and what he sets out to do will come to pass. Neither will God ever change anything he has promised. His promises are as good as done the second he makes them.

We see a hint of this in Numbers 23. An enemy of God's people named Balak tried to get a man named Balaam to curse Israel. But God had Balaam bless Israel instead. When Balak got angry, Balaam told him he couldn't curse the people when God had blessed them. There was no way he could change God's mind about it. God is simply unchanging.

This might not sound like the most amazing of God's attributes, but it's quite important. Because God doesn't change, that means he's completely dependable. He won't run out of power. He won't run out of love. And whatever he's said he will do (like bless Israel in Numbers 23), we can trust him to do. God has said that whoever believes in Jesus is forgiven of sin and will live with him forever. Because God is unchanging, we can be absolutely sure he will make good on that wonderful promise!

▶ *What changes make you feel anxious? Excited?*

WHAT DOES IT MEAN THAT GOD IS IMMUTABLE?

▶ How much of yourself would you change if you could?

1—2—3—4—5—6—7—8—9—10

NOTHING   EVERYTHING

▶ What questions do you have so far?

▶ What are you wondering about because of what you've heard?

PRAYER

God, thank you for never changing and being completely dependable in who you are and what you do. Amen.

FAMILY ACTIVITY: OBSERVE

Do it. Look at family pictures going as far back as possible. Notice how your family has changed. Identify the good changes and any not-so-good ones.

Discuss it. Talk about how sometimes our changes are good and sometimes our changes aren't quite good.

Connect it. Share that God never changes. He's the best ever, just as he always has been and always will be.

▼ JESUS CONNECTION ▼

The good news about Jesus being God and unchanging is we know exactly who we're trying to become like. As we grow in love like Jesus, we know he won't change anything about his love. And the same is true of his other perfect human characteristics. Because of this, we can be sure of how we want to live, and with God's help we'll get closer and closer to it each day.

▶ *Which characteristic of Jesus will you try to display today?*

14

IS GOD PERFECT?

Yes. God is perfect in all his attributes and ways and he lacks nothing.

DEUTERONOMY 32:3-4 (OR 32:4)

Are you good at bottle flipping? How about flipping a coin? How many times in a row do you think you could flip a bottle and make it stand up or make a coin land on heads? What about making basketball free throws or soccer free kicks?

That's how we tend to think of God's perfection—never making a mistake. And that's true. God is perfect in that way; he never makes a mistake. That's what Moses told the Israelites in Deuteronomy 32. Everything God does is perfect. But God's perfection is even more than that. Not only is God perfect in all his characteristics and ways, but he also lacks nothing. To be perfect is to be complete. So God acts in love every time he does something, but more than that, he is perfectly love. He never shows us fifty percent love, or ninety percent love, or even ninety-nine percent love. He loves us completely. And there's nothing we could add to God to make him more loving or better in any other way.

If that's hard to understand, perhaps an illustration will help. Imagine you took a twenty-question test on your favorite musician. If you got all twenty questions correct, that would be a perfect score, right? But would that mean you know everything about that musician? Not at all! Getting a perfect score on that test doesn't mean you have perfect knowledge of that musician. When we talk about God being perfect, it's not just that he would get a perfect score, but he'd also know every other detail there is to know. His knowledge is perfect in that way. And so is everything else about him. God is perfect; there's not even the tiniest way he could improve.

▶ *What would your perfect day look like?*

IS GOD PERFECT?

▶ How perfect are you at obeying God?

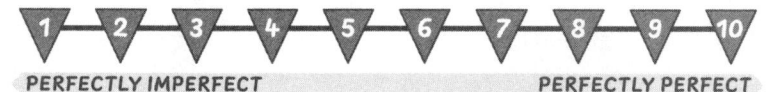

1 — 2 — 3 — 4 — 5 — 6 — 7 — 8 — 9 — 10

PERFECTLY IMPERFECT   PERFECTLY PERFECT

▶ What questions do you have so far?

▶ What are you wondering about because of what you've heard?

PRAYER

God, thank you that you are perfect in all your ways so we can trust you fully. Amen.

FAMILY ACTIVITY: COMPETE

Do it. Flip bottles, shoot free throws, flip a coin, or participate in some other challenge to see who can succeed the most times in a row. Then work together as a team to do as many in a row as possible.

Discuss it. Talk about how hard it is for us to be perfect like that even in small ways.

Connect it. Share that God is perfect in all his ways.

▼ JESUS CONNECTION ▼

Jesus shows us what it looks like to be perfect in two important ways. First, Jesus never sinned. Not even once. Second, Jesus obeyed God the Father perfectly—every single time and in every single way. For now, we can't be perfect in either of those ways, but we can recognize that God sees us as perfect and we can live in ways to please God because of what Jesus has done.

▶ How can you turn away from sin and love God more this week?

15 IS ANYONE OR ANYTHING GREATER THAN GOD?

No. God is greater than everyone and everything.

ISAIAH 44:13-20 (OR 44:16-18)

What is your greatest treasure? What one thing is worth the most to you? Perhaps it's something that costs a lot, or perhaps it's something you simply care the most about. Perhaps it's a pet or a person. Whatever it is, it's good that you like it. It's even good if you love it. But what you don't want to do is make that person, pet, or thing your greatest treasure even above God. That top spot of being the absolute greatest belongs to God alone. It's actually pretty foolish to put anything else in God's top spot. This is what we see throughout the Old Testament.

In the Old Testament, people worshiped idols—carved statues that represented different gods. These gods weren't real, of course. Only God is real. But in their foolishness, people worshiped these idols as gods instead of the one true God. So at one point, God told the prophet Jeremiah how silly this was. People would take a piece of wood, burn part of it to keep warm, then carve the other part and worship it. What they worshiped could just as easily have gone into the fire! What kind of god is that?

We might not worship little carved idols, but any time we place anything over God, we make it into a different kind of idol. And when we do that, we're being just as foolish as those people in the Old Testament. Our amazing God is truly our greatest treasure. It's good to have other treasures; God has given them to us to enjoy. But we always need to keep those treasures in the right priority. God must always be first!

▶ *What are some idols people have today?*

IS ANYONE OR ANYTHING GREATER THAN GOD? 37

▶ **Is God always in your top spot?**

1 — 2 — 3 — 4 — 5 — 6 — 7 — 8 — 9 — 10

I'VE GOT LOTS OF IDOLS　　　　　GOD ALWAYS COMES FIRST

▶ **What questions do you have so far?**

▶ **What are you wondering about because of what you've heard?**

PRAYER

God, thank you for being our greatest treasure and for giving us so many other good things too. Amen.

FAMILY ACTIVITY: PLAY

Do it. Create a treasure hunt. Hide a treasure, preferably one your family can enjoy immediately once it's found. Then, create several clues, each leading to the next clue and the last one leading to the treasure.

Discuss it. Talk about the things you treasure and what people in the world often treasure.

Connect it. Share how God has given us wonderful gifts, but none is greater than him.

▼ JESUS CONNECTION ▼

It's fun to talk about our treasures. Nothing, though, is more fun than talking about our greatest treasure: God. Why wouldn't we want to tell our friends and others about how wonderful God is? This is what Jesus did during his time on earth. Every opportunity he had, Jesus told people about how amazing the Father is, and he invited them to love and follow him.

▶ **Who can you tell about God this week?**

16 HOW MUCH AUTHORITY DOES GOD HAVE?

God has all authority and rules over his creation perfectly with loving care.

PSALM 115:1-8 (OR 115:3)

Have you ever pretended to be a king or queen? Perhaps you ordered your gallant knights to slay a fierce dragon or led them on some other wonderful adventure. While you and your friends played, it might have seemed like you were in charge, but you weren't really. Your friends did only what they wanted to do. And it probably didn't take long for someone to declare it was his turn to be king or her turn to be queen, and just like that, you lost your throne.

This shows us that saying you're in charge doesn't really mean you're in charge. To truly be in charge takes authority: the right to do what you want. If you don't have authority, you're not really a ruler. At the same time, rulers need something else just as much: power. Without power, you might lose your authority! That's why kings and queens often had big strong armies to protect their kingdoms.

God is our perfect ruler because he has both limitless authority and limitless power. That's what Psalm 115 talks about. God is our true King who does whatever he pleases, and we know he is all-powerful too, so nothing can resist him. That means no enemy can defeat him ever! But we have no reason to be afraid of such an all-powerful God with all authority. That's because God loves us. God rules over us perfectly with loving care for us. Our God of limitless authority and limitless power has limitless love for you!

▶ *If you were king or queen for a day, what would you do?*

▶ How willing are you to follow God as your King?

1 — 2 — 3 — 4 — 5 — 6 — 7 — 8 — 9 — 10
I REFUSE   FULLY AND ALWAYS

▶ What questions do you have so far?

▶ What are you wondering about because of what you've heard?

PRAYER

God, thank you for being a perfect King who loves us, cares for us, provides for us, and protects us. Amen.

FAMILY ACTIVITY: EXPLORE

Do it. Visit a local town hall or a city, state, or national government building.

Discuss it. Talk about what goes on in that building and some of the leaders who have served there.

Connect it. Share how even the best of human leaders aren't perfect, but God is our perfect King.

▼ JESUS CONNECTION ▼

Jesus is God and has all authority and power. But while he was on earth, Jesus willingly obeyed the Father in all things. In doing this, Jesus shows us the perfect example of humble, joyful obedience to our King. God the Father is the best King there is. He cares for us and protects us and he sent Jesus to earth so we can be forgiven. Why wouldn't we want to love and obey such a great King?

▶ What is one way you will obey God your King this week?

PART 2

JESUS

The name *Jesus* doesn't appear in the Bible until the New Testament (although *Joshua*, basically the Hebrew version of that name, does). Because of this, some people think that Jesus didn't exist until he was born in Bethlehem around 6 or 5 BC. But that's not correct. Jesus is the Son of God, which means he's fully God, and that means he's eternal.

This is the important point the apostle John wanted to make as he opened his Gospel account: "In the beginning was the Word [Jesus], and the Word [Jesus] was with God, and the Word [Jesus] was fully God" (John 1:1). The manger in Bethlehem wasn't where Jesus came into being; it was where the eternal Son of God, wrapped in human flesh, came into the world.

In this section, you'll work through several key truths about Jesus, a field of theology called *Christology*. As you do, be sure to keep Jesus being both fully God and fully human at the front of your mind. There's a mystery to it, for sure. The idea of God becoming human and being limited as a person is a head-scratcher. But it's critical that we help our kids understand that Jesus is, always has been, and always will be fully God, and then two thousand years ago he became fully human. If we remove or reduce either, we don't teach who Jesus really is. He isn't God who is kind of a human; neither is he a human who is kind of God. He's the God-man. One hundred percent God, one hundred percent human. We might not be able to understand how both these truths fit together (a doctrine called *the hypostatic union*), but our job is to teach that they both are true.

The questions about Jesus in this section also draw our attention to what he did for us on the cross. His miracles and teachings matter, of course. His miracles prove his identity and his teachings point us to what God's kingdom is like. And they both show his great love for people. But as much as those words and works matter, Jesus came to do even more than that; he came to lay down his life on our behalf. It's only through Jesus' perfect life, sacrificial death, and triumphant resurrection that we can find forgiveness of our sins. But there's one other core idea covered in this section that we can't miss: the change we experience when we trust in Jesus. When we trust in Jesus, we become new creations and we're given a new identity in him. And because of this, we're able to live like Jesus—imitating his perfect human characteristics. This idea is foundational to what will be covered in part seven on Christian living.

17 HAS GOD THE SON ALWAYS EXISTED?

Yes. God the Son has always existed, just as God the Father and God the Holy Spirit have.

JOHN 1:1-4 (OR 1:1)

John was a good friend and faithful follower of Jesus who wanted to help others become Jesus' friends and followers too. That's why when John was an older man, he wrote a Gospel—a true story about who Jesus is and what he did. John began his Gospel with three very interesting words: "In the beginning." What's so special about that? Well, that's exactly how Genesis, the first book of the Bible, begins. And there's a really good reason John connected his story of Jesus to the beginning of everything. He wanted us to know that Jesus is God the Son, who has existed forever just like God the Father and God the Holy Spirit. John wanted us to know that to understand the whole story of Jesus, you have to go a lot further back than a baby born in Bethlehem.

You see, some of the first people who read John's Gospel had been alive when Jesus was alive, about sixty years earlier. They had seen a human being, but John wanted them to understand that Jesus is more than a human being; he's the eternal Son of God. So John pointed his readers back to Genesis and he called Jesus "the Word." That might sound odd until we remember how everything was created—by God's spoken word! John then said that all things were created by Jesus, the Word, including light and life.

Jesus is the Word, the Son of God who has existed forever just like God the Father and God the Spirit. And just like he was part of creating life in the very beginning, he gives new life to anyone who trusts in him!

▶ **What questions about Jesus being the eternal Son of God do you have?**

HAS GOD THE SON ALWAYS EXISTED?

▶ How much sense does Jesus being the eternal Son of God make to you?

1 — 2 — 3 — 4 — 5 — 6 — 7 — 8 — 9 — 10
IT REALLY DOESN'T   IT TOTALLY DOES

▶ What questions do you have so far?

▶ What are you wondering about because of what you've heard?

PRAYER

God, thank you for creating us and giving us life, and thank you for providing Jesus so we can have new life in him. Amen.

FAMILY ACTIVITY: EXPLORE

Do it. Visit a new house or building being constructed, or watch an online video of something being built.

Discuss it. Talk about what house features you like the most and what parts of the building process you find most interesting.

Connect it. Share how everything, like that house, has a beginning, but Jesus does not. He is the Son of God, who has lived for eternity.

▼ JESUS CONNECTION ▼

Jesus is the eternal Son of God, who came to earth for a very important reason: to give life to all who believe in him. When we trust that Jesus is God, that he gave up his life and then was raised from the dead, we are forgiven of all our sins and we are promised a wonderful life forever with Jesus and all others who have trusted in him.

▶ How can you thank Jesus for the life he's given and celebrate his wonderful gift?

18

WHAT IS THE INCARNATION?

The incarnation is when God the Son came to earth to live as a human.

LUKE 2:1-20 (OR 2:6-7)

Jesus is God the Son and has always existed. So what happened in Bethlehem then? Well, about two thousand years ago, Mary was given a son to grow within her, and that son was born about nine months later in the town of Bethlehem. But all of this wasn't Jesus' beginning; rather, it was when he began to exist as a human. Jesus, the Son of God, has existed forever in spirit form, but when he began growing within Mary just like other children grow within their mothers, he became a person made of flesh and bones too. This is what the word *incarnation* means: "in the flesh." The Son of God becoming human is a great mystery of our faith, just like the Trinity. How could an eternal, perfect, infinite God become a human? We can't be sure how it happened, but we can be completely sure that it *did* happen.

After Jesus was born, he grew up and fulfilled many of the Old Testament prophecies showing that he is the Rescuer first promised in Genesis 3:15. When Adam and Eve sinned, God told them that one day he would send someone to defeat sin and death. This Rescuer would be special and do what no one else could do. Jesus' teachings and miracles proved he is that Rescuer. Jesus is the Son of God who became a human to live a perfect life, give up his life for us, and then rise victoriously from the dead!

This is the mysterious and wonderful truth we celebrate at Christmas. We do many fun things at Christmas, but we don't want to ever forget that the heart of the season's celebration is how the Son of God came to earth and was born as a baby.

▶ *What are some of your favorite things about Christmas?*

WHAT IS THE INCARNATION?

▶ How difficult is it for you to understand that the Son of God was born as a baby boy?

1 — 2 — 3 — 4 — 5 — 6 — 7 — 8 — 9 — 10
I'M TOTALLY LOST　　　　　　　　　　　　THIS IS EASY-PEASY

▶ What questions do you have so far?

▶ What are you wondering about because of what you've heard?

PRAYER

God, thank you for Jesus, the Son of God, coming to earth to be born in such a humble way. Amen.

FAMILY ACTIVITY: CELEBRATE

Do it. No matter what time of the year it is, celebrate Christmas. Go all out and decorate, make favorite treats, listen to music, give gifts, and dress as if it were Christmastime.

Discuss it. Talk about your favorite parts of Christmas and the traditions you love or would like to begin.

Connect it. Share how we might celebrate Jesus' birth one time a year, but it's something we can celebrate always.

▼ JESUS CONNECTION ▼

Can you imagine being a king but living like a common peasant? That's like what Jesus did when he came to earth. He left a throne surrounded by angels in heaven to be born in something like a barn surrounded by animals. And in doing this, Jesus shows us the perfect example of living with humility—always putting the Father and others first. When we think of what Jesus did, can anything be too lowly for us to do?

▶ How can you demonstrate Jesus-like humility this week?

19

WHY DID GOD THE SON BECOME HUMAN?

God the Son became fully human while remaining fully God to live a perfect life, and then to be a perfect sacrifice and rise from the dead to provide forgiveness of sin.

PHILIPPIANS 2:5-11 (OR 2:8)

It can be difficult to understand *how* Jesus is the eternal Son of God who became human, but it's not as difficult to understand *why* he did. There are two big reasons.

First, Jesus became human to live in perfect obedience to the Father. Because of our sin, we disobey God in many ways. Some are big; some are small. Some are on purpose; some are by accident. Even after we trust in Jesus, we still can't fully obey God. We still mess up and fall short. It's true that we will grow in obedience, but we will always disobey to some degree. But not Jesus. He did what we cannot do by completely obeying the Father. And that takes us to the second reason Jesus became a human.

In Philippians 2:8, Paul tells us Jesus obeyed the Father even to the point of dying on a cross. That's how Jesus paid the penalty of sin that we owed. Disobeying God leads to death (Genesis 2:17; Romans 6:23). On the cross, Jesus died in our place to take the punishment for our sins. He then rose from the dead, showing he is victorious. But to do all this, he first had to become human. Human sin earns human death. None of the animal sacrifices in the Old Testament could pay this penalty. That's why people kept sacrificing over and over again. Those sacrifices didn't solve their sin problem; they pointed to Jesus, the perfect once-and-for-all sacrifice who would come one day and solve it once and for all.

Had Jesus sinned even once, he couldn't have been the perfect sacrifice given in our place. Jesus' perfect life made this possible and it gives us the perfect example of obedience to follow.

▶ Would you rather have lived in Old Testament times sacrificing animals or today? Why?

WHY DID GOD THE SON BECOME HUMAN?

▶ **How good are you at following Jesus' example of obedience?**

1 — 2 — 3 — 4 — 5 — 6 — 7 — 8 — 9 — 10

I MESS UP ALL THE TIME   I'M AN EXPERT

▶ **What questions do you have so far?**

▶ **What are you wondering about because of what you've heard?**

PRAYER

God, thank you for Jesus coming to live a perfect life, giving up his life, and then rising from the dead to provide forgiveness for our sins. Amen.

FAMILY ACTIVITY: SERVE

Do it. Serve in a shelter or make and distribute care packages for the homeless.

Discuss it. Talk about the experience. What was uncomfortable or challenging? What was rewarding?

Connect it. Share that serving in this way might be uncomfortable, but it's one way we can follow Jesus' example. It wasn't easy for Jesus to come to earth, but he did. Obeying God isn't always easy, but it's always worth it.

▼ JESUS CONNECTION ▼

Jesus' perfect life of obedience is an example for us to follow in many ways, but perhaps one of the most important ways is forgiveness. Jesus obeyed the Father so people could be forgiven of their sins. We can't forgive the wrong someone does toward God. But we can forgive others whenever they do wrong to us. To live like Jesus is to live with forgiveness for small things and big things.

▶ **Who do you need to forgive and how will you do that?**

20

WHAT DID JESUS DO WHILE HE WAS ON THE EARTH?

While Jesus was on the earth, he traveled throughout Galilee, Samaria, and Judea, teaching and performing miracles.

MATTHEW 4:17-25 (OR 4:23)

We don't know much about when Jesus was a boy. We know about his birth and one story from when he was twelve years old at the temple, but we don't really meet Jesus until he was about thirty years old. From that point, the four Gospels describe Jesus' ministry lasting from about AD 27–30. During those three and a half years, Jesus mainly traveled throughout three regions—Galilee, Samaria, and Judea—although he did cross into other areas at times. Matthew 4 gives us a snapshot of what Jesus did during those travels: he taught and performed miracles.

It didn't take long for Jesus' teachings and miracles to draw big crowds. Something about the way he taught fascinated people. His teaching had authority, unlike many other teachers of that day. But his miracles grew his fame even more than his teachings did. Jesus didn't perform these miracles to be popular, though. Every miracle he did was to honor and glorify the Father and to prove his identity as the Son of God. The goal was for people to see these miracles, recognize that they couldn't be done by any "regular" person, and then listen to Jesus' teachings about himself so they would recognize him as the Rescuer, also called the Messiah or the Christ.

But there was still another reason for these miracles. Many of them—such as feeding hungry people and healing hurting people—were done out of Jesus' great love and compassion for people. He saw people in need and took care of those needs. No one was just a "prop" Jesus used for his own purposes. Jesus truly and deeply cared for each and every person he fed and healed. And he lovingly cares for you the same way.

▶ *Which of Jesus' miracles would you most like to have seen in person?*

WHAT DID JESUS DO WHILE HE WAS ON THE EARTH?

▶ Which helps you believe that Jesus is the Son of God more: his teachings or his miracles?

1—2—3—4—5—6—7—8—9—10
TEACHINGS   MIRACLES

▶ What questions do you have so far?

▶ What are you wondering about because of what you've heard?

PRAYER

God, thank you that Jesus taught us how to be your friend and that his miracles show us who he is and how much he loves us. Amen.

FAMILY ACTIVITY: EXPERIMENT

Do it. Search online for how to do a few magic tricks. Then hold a family magic show.

Discuss it. Talk about how magic tricks aren't real—they usually rely on optical illusions to fool the audience.

Connect it. Share how Jesus' miracles weren't tricks or illusions. They were all real, and they each prove his identity and show his amazing power.

▼ JESUS CONNECTION ▼

We might not be able to teach or do miracles like Jesus did, but we can care for people like he did. Hurting and needy people are all around us, but sometimes we miss them because we aren't looking. This is why it helps to slow down and pay more attention to what is around us. Many of the people we see need physical care, but they all need to know Jesus.

▶ How can you slow down to see others around you and perhaps help someone in need?

21

WHAT DID JESUS DO TO RESCUE US FROM OUR SINS?

Jesus rescued us from our sins by dying on the cross as the perfect sacrifice and then rising from the dead on the third day.

ROMANS 5:6-11 (OR 5:8)

Romans 5:8 tells us that because God loves us, Jesus came to earth to be our Rescuer by dying for our sins. We've never been more loved or given a greater gift than that! Jesus paid a punishment he didn't deserve and suffered death on a Roman cross. But that's not all he did for us. His act of forgiveness began before that when he became a human. The punishment for sin is death—a human death—so the Son of God had to become a human to be a worthy substitute for that punishment.

Jesus lived just over thirty years never sinning and always obeying the Father. This, too, was essential, because it proves that Jesus is a pure, worthy sacrifice. This is why in the Old Testament animals had to be spotless to be worthy sacrifices. They were supposed to be as perfect as possible. Why? Because they pictured the sacrifice God would later provide in Jesus.

While the sacrificial animals were to be perfect on the outside, Jesus was better than that; he was perfect on the inside. He was without sin. Never once in his life did Jesus lie. Or steal. Or covet. Or take advantage of someone. Or be prideful or selfish. That's why he was our worthy substitute on the cross. A sinful person can't pay the punishment for other sinful people. But sinless Jesus could, and he did!

The act of dying on the cross is the core of how Jesus provided forgiveness of sin. But Jesus didn't stay dead. On the third day, Jesus rose from the dead showing that he had won the victory over sin! When we trust in who Jesus is and what Jesus did, we are rescued from all our sins.

▶ If you could be perfect at just one thing, what would it be?

WHAT DID JESUS DO TO RESCUE US FROM OUR SINS?

▶ **How thankful are you for Jesus' forgiveness of your sins?**

1 — 2 — 3 — 4 — 5 — 6 — 7 — 8 — 9 — 10

WHATEVER   AMAZED

▶ **What questions do you have so far?**

▶ **What are you wondering about because of what you've heard?**

PRAYER

God, thank you for Jesus coming to be our perfect Rescuer to provide the one and only way to be forgiven of our sins. Amen.

FAMILY ACTIVITY: BLESS

Do it. Go out for ice cream or some other treat. If you are able, pay for a stranger or leave a larger tip than normal. Otherwise, find another way to be generous toward someone.

Discuss it. Talk about ways you can live with increased generosity and kindness.

Connect it. Share how our small acts of kindness picture the amazing act of God's kindness to us in providing Jesus to pay for our sins.

▼ JESUS CONNECTION ▼

When we trust in Jesus as our Rescuer, we're completely forgiven by God the Father. But that doesn't mean we never sin again. Sadly, we still do. These sins are forgiven, but that doesn't mean they don't matter. Sin never pleases God and it's never good for us. When we sin, it's best to turn from sin, celebrate God's love and forgiveness, and set our minds and hearts to live in obedience like Jesus.

▶ **What will you do the next time you sin?**

22

WHAT HAPPENED ON THE THIRD DAY AFTER JESUS DIED ON THE CROSS?

On the third day, Jesus rose from the dead, left the grave, and was seen by many witnesses.

JOHN 20:11-20 (OR 20:20)

Jesus was on the cross for hours, then he breathed his last and died. There was no doubt he was dead—the Roman soldiers made sure of it. Jesus' body was then taken down from the cross, wrapped in burial cloth, and placed in a tomb. But Jesus didn't stay dead. On Sunday morning, the third day (Friday was day one, Saturday was day two, and Sunday was day three), Jesus was raised back to life. In an instant, a burial tomb became an empty tomb! Jesus' resurrection shows he has the power to defeat death—his and ours.

At first there was confusion about the empty tomb. Some of Jesus' followers like Mary Magdalene thought someone had moved Jesus' body or that grave robbers had taken it. But Mary's confusion and sadness turned to amazement and joy when Jesus appeared to her.

Jesus appeared to many others, too, proving he is alive and filling his disciples with hope. Jesus appeared to two women (Matthew 28:1-10), two disciples on the road to Emmaus (Luke 24:13-32), the disciples (John 20:19-31), more than five hundred people at once (1 Corinthians 15:6), and James and all the apostles (1 Corinthians 15:7). These witnesses helped prove that Jesus was dead, but he is now alive. Many had seen the crucifixion, and when they saw the resurrected Jesus, they saw the wounds on his body. There was no doubt that this was the same Jesus who had died. He is alive indeed! This is the greatest news of all!

Jesus spent forty days after his resurrection appearing to people to prove he is alive and to prepare them to continue the mission he began. Then, he returned to heaven (Acts 1:9).

▶ **What do you think it felt like for Jesus' followers to see him alive again?**

WHAT HAPPENED ON THE THIRD DAY AFTER JESUS DIED?

▶ How certain are you that Jesus rose from the dead?

1 — 2 — 3 — 4 — 5 — 6 — 7 — 8 — 9 — 10

I REALLY DOUBT IT .... I'M SURE OF IT

▶ What questions do you have so far?

▶ What are you wondering about because of what you've heard?

PRAYER

God, thank you for the witnesses who saw Jesus' resurrection so we can have a faith that isn't blind but rather one that's based on plenty of evidence. Amen.

FAMILY ACTIVITY: CELEBRATE

Do it. No matter what time of year it is, celebrate Easter. Go all out and decorate, dress up, and enjoy a special Easter meal. Perhaps invite family, friends, and neighbors over.

Discuss it. Talk about your favorite parts of Easter and the traditions you love or would like to begin.

Connect it. Share how we might celebrate Jesus' resurrection one time a year in particular, but it's something we can celebrate always.

▼ JESUS CONNECTION ▼

Can you imagine the disciples' smiles when they saw Jesus alive again? What an amazing celebration that must have been! We often think about God wanting us to obey him, but we can't miss that he wants us to have joy just as much. He wants us to experience the most amazing, fulfilling, joyful life there is. Jesus lived with joy and brought joy to others, and we can do the same.

▶ *What can you do to be joyful and bring joy to someone else this week?*

23

WHAT DOES IT MEAN TO BECOME A NEW CREATION IN CHRIST?

To become a new creation in Christ means to be given a new identity in Christ; the old has gone and the new has come.

2 CORINTHIANS 5:14-17 (OR 5:17)

Something amazing happens the moment you finish the last grade of elementary school. Just like that—in the blink of an eye—you're no longer an elementary schooler; you've become a middle schooler. One second you weren't a middle schooler and the next second you are. The same is true when you move from middle school to high school. Or when you make a sports team or earn a spot in a drama performance or join a band. In a split second you become a soccer player, an actor, or a musician.

All these changes are great and important in their own ways, but none are as wonderful or as important as what happens the second you trust in Jesus. In that split second, you become a brand-new person. You have been made new in Christ.

This is what Paul had in mind when he wrote 2 Corinthians 5. He wanted the church at Corinth, and us, to understand that trusting in Jesus doesn't mean we're slightly changed; it means we're completely changed. This enormous change concerns our relationship with God. Before trusting in Jesus, we were unforgiven, sinful people who deserved God's judgment. But the split second we trust in Jesus, that's all gone. Instead, we become forgiven, holy people who have been given God's amazing grace. We've gone from being strangers to being part of our loving God's family.

It's an amazing change, one that is completely for the better. We might not look different or feel different. It might not seem like much has changed on the outside of us, but in reality, we have experienced a most amazing, wonderful change within us. All thanks to Jesus!

▶ *What is one thing you'd like to change about yourself?*

WHAT DOES IT MEAN TO BECOME A NEW CREATION?

▶ How do feel about being made brand new in Jesus?

1 — 2 — 3 — 4 — 5 — 6 — 7 — 8 — 9 — 10
IT FRIGHTENS ME   IT EXCITES ME

▶ What questions do you have so far?

▶ What are you wondering about because of what you've heard?

PRAYER

God, thank you for making us into new creations through our faith in Jesus. Amen.

FAMILY ACTIVITY: CREATE

Do it. Collect unused items or junk. Work together to make something new, such as a piece of art, out of those old items.

Discuss it. As you work, talk about how you are making old, broken, useless things beautiful again.

Connect it. Share how God has done to us what we've done in our project, only better. We were always loved by God, but we were broken because of our sin. Jesus came to provide us with forgiveness and make us new!

▼ JESUS CONNECTION ▼

Because Jesus became fully human, he understands what life is like for us. He knows it's difficult at times. But because of what he's done for us and because of the gift of the Holy Spirit we've been given within us, we have the power to live in obedience to God. We can't live perfectly like Jesus, but with his help we can get closer to that each day.

▶ With the Spirit's help, how can you be like Jesus and obey God in whatever you do today?

24

WHAT DOES IT MEAN TO HAVE A NEW IDENTITY IN CHRIST?

To have a new identity in Christ means the core of who we are has changed; we have been re-created to live the way God made us.

GALATIANS 2:20-21 (OR 2:20)

Who are you? The way you answer this question helps explain your identity. While there are many different parts of your identity, only one part is most important and defines you the best. You might be an athlete or a musician, but that's not your truest identity. You might be a student or a friend. But that's not your truest identity either. You might be a son or a daughter and a sister or a brother. As important as these are, they still aren't your truest identity.

If you have trusted in Jesus, your truest identity is the new creation you have become in him. The other parts of your identity aren't unimportant, but they aren't most important either. Being made new in Jesus is. That's your core identity. That's the best way to understand who you really are.

Having trusted in Jesus, you've been made new in Jesus so you can live like Jesus. That's what Paul had in mind when he wrote Galatians 2:20. Jesus' identity has become your identity and his actions are to become your actions. We can't go too far with this idea, though. Jesus is God; we aren't and never will be. That means Jesus can do things we can't do. For example, we'll never be all-knowing or all-powerful like Jesus. We'll always be limited in these ways.

So as we look to Jesus to see how we are to live, we don't look at his perfect divine nature; we look at his perfect human nature. With God's help, that's what we set as our goal to copy in full. And with God's help that's what we can do. We can live more like our amazing Rescuer and friend, Jesus, with each passing day.

▶ *What are some different parts of your identity?*

WHAT DOES IT MEAN TO HAVE A NEW IDENTITY IN CHRIST?

▶ *How much do you think you live like Jesus?*

1 — 2 — 3 — 4 — 5 — 6 — 7 — 8 — 9 — 10

NOT AT ALL   EXACTLY

▶ *What questions do you have so far?*

▶ *What are you wondering about because of what you've heard?*

PRAYER

God, thank you for changing us and giving us a new priceless identity in Jesus. Amen.

FAMILY ACTIVITY: PLAY

Do it. Play the board game Guess Who? or make up and play a game like it.

Discuss it. Talk about what makes people different and how these differences are good.

Connect it. Share how God has made us with different characteristics, identities, and personalities and that's always good, but no matter how we're different, we can each look like Jesus.

▼ JESUS CONNECTION ▼

It takes humility to live like Jesus. We must recognize that the other parts of our identity—like being an athlete or student—are wonderful, but they aren't as important as our new identity in Jesus. Living like him comes first. We don't have to find this humility on our own, though. We can turn to Jesus for an example of that too. Jesus lived in perfect humility, always putting the Father first and others second.

▶ *What are some ways you can show others Jesus-like humility this week?*

25 HOW ARE WE ABLE TO LIVE LIKE JESUS?

We are able to live like Jesus and imitate his perfect human character by the power of the Holy Spirit who is within us

ACTS 1:6-11 (OR 1:8)

To imitate something is to copy it. Imitation vanilla is made to taste just like real vanilla. Imitation leather is made to look and feel just like real leather. In the same way, we're to be imitations of Jesus. We're to copy him as exactly as we can.

The best place to see how to do this is the four Gospels: Matthew, Mark, Luke, and John. We read these books not just to understand how Jesus came to die for our sins—although that's incredibly important, of course! We also read them to see what it means to live the way God made us to live. We look at the love of Jesus and see love for us and love we are to show others. The same is true of his obedience, humility, compassion, generosity, forgiveness, and much more. Living like this is our calling and goal.

How do we do this, though? How can we hope to come even close to living like Jesus? First, we can do this only if we've trusted in Jesus and been made new. But even then it's not automatic. Here's the wonderful thing: God doesn't leave us on our own to live like Jesus; he's given us the Holy Spirit to change us, guide us, and direct us! This is how Jesus told his first followers they'd be able to continue his mission. They couldn't do it on their own and they weren't expected to. They needed the Holy Spirit. We do too. With our eyes fixed on Jesus and in the power of the Holy Spirit, we can live the way we were made to live: like Jesus.

▶ **Which character trait of Jesus do you most appreciate and love?**

HOW ARE WE ABLE TO LIVE LIKE JESUS?

▶ How comfortable are you letting the Holy Spirit change you and guide you to be like Jesus?

1 — 2 — 3 — 4 — 5 — 6 — 7 — 8 — 9 — 10

THAT'S SCARY!   THAT'S FANTASTIC!

▶ What questions do you have so far?

▶ What are you wondering about because of what you've heard?

PRAYER

God, thank you for giving us the Holy Spirit to change us and help us live more like Jesus. Amen.

FAMILY ACTIVITY: EXPERIMENT

Do it. Purchase the name brand and store brand of several items and see who can figure out which is which.

Discuss it. Talk about how store brands try to imitate name brands, sometimes coming close but not always.

Connect it. Share how we can be just like Jesus with the Holy Spirit's help.

▼ JESUS CONNECTION ▼

When we humbly allow the Holy Spirit to guide us and empower us, we're living like Jesus. He, too, was led by the Holy Spirit during his earthly ministry, like when the Spirit led him into the wilderness after his baptism. Living like Jesus in this way is the key to living like him in every other way.

▶ How can you let the Holy Spirit guide you to be more like Jesus today?

PART 3

THE HOLY SPIRIT

CAN WE BE HONEST? Life is hard at times. Following Jesus can be too. Sometimes it can even feel like following Jesus *makes* life hard. We know it, and our kids know it too. Jesus never promised that following him would be the path to comfort and ease. He promised that it would be challenging. He promised that it would be difficult. He even promised that it would be painful at times. But we can't miss something else Jesus promised: he promised that we won't make this journey alone. The Holy Spirit will always be with us.

In this section, we'll dive into the study of the Holy Spirit, or *pneumatology*. The first question concerns *who* the Holy Spirit is. The word *who* is emphasized because that's crucial to understanding the Holy Spirit. He is a "he," not an "it." He is a person, just like God the Father and God the Son. And just like God the Father and God the Son, the Holy Spirit is fully God.

The rest of the questions then concern what the Holy Spirit does—how he comes alongside us to help us. This makes all the difference as we navigate the challenges of life. Jesus didn't tell us life would be hard and then leave us with a "good luck" and a thumbs-up. He left us with one of the three persons of the Trinity coming to live within us when we trust in Christ. The Holy Spirit is ever-present, providing comfort, care, guidance, assurance, and much more. The Holy Spirit will carry us through any difficulty we face.

But just like the beauty and power of the cross are true for us only if we trust in Jesus, we must recognize that the ministry of the Holy Spirit means little if we fail to live in humility. He is always with us, but we need to always be giving him control of our lives so he will do what he wants to do and is capable of doing for us. We need to yield to the Holy Spirit or, put another way, live by the Spirit and give him room to work in us, through us, and for us.

The Holy Spirit is one of God's greatest gifts to us. He is there ready to lead us, guide us, and help us. He's also ready to produce his fruit in us—fruit that is good for us and for others. But it all hinges on us, in humility, trusting in Jesus and being changed by him, then continuing in humility day by day as we turn control of our lives over to God the Holy Spirit.

26 IS THE HOLY SPIRIT A PERSON?

Yes. The Holy Spirit is a person, just like God the Father and God the Son.

EPHESIANS 4:29-32 (OR 4:30)

We hear quite a lot about God the Father and God the Son, but we don't seem to hear about God the Holy Spirit as much. Many Christians don't know what he does; some don't even know he's God. One common belief is that the Holy Spirit is a "force," which is why people often refer to the Holy Spirit as "it" instead of "him." But that isn't correct. The Holy Spirit isn't a "force" or an "it." He's a "he." He's a person, one of the three persons of the Godhead along with the Father and Son. Just like God the Father and God the Son are persons because they think, feel, and make choices, so is God the Spirit.

In Ephesians 4, we're told that we need to be careful with the words we use and that we shouldn't be bitter or angry. Instead, we're to be compassionate and forgiving to one another. In the middle of these instructions, we're told something else: we aren't to grieve the Holy Spirit. To grieve someone is to cause that person great sadness and trouble. It's to hurt someone deeply. So we're not supposed to do things that would cause the Holy Spirit to feel sadness and trouble.

That means the Holy Spirit must be a person; a "force" doesn't feel anything. Only persons feel. This, along with the Holy Spirit thinking (Romans 8:27) and making choices (1 Corinthians 12:11) shows us that the Holy Spirit is a person, just like the Father and Son.

▶ *What are some things that make you feel sad or troubled?*

IS THE HOLY SPIRIT A PERSON?

▶ How much do you know about the Holy Spirit?

1 — 2 — 3 — 4 — 5 — 6 — 7 — 8 — 9 — 10

A BLANK PAGE　　　　　　　　　　　　NOTEBOOKS FULL OF INFO

▶ What questions do you have so far?

▶ What are you wondering about because of what you've heard?

PRAYER

God, thank you for being bigger than we can understand at times but also for helping us know all we need to know about you. Amen.

FAMILY ACTIVITY: EXPERIMENT

Do it. Experiment with magnets. Feel the magnetic force between them and attempt to pick up heavy objects with them.

Discuss it. As you experiment, talk about how a magnetic force can attract or repel things.

Connect it. Share how the Holy Spirit isn't a force like a magnetic force; he is a person we can know, love, and follow.

▼ JESUS CONNECTION ▼

During his time on earth, Jesus relied on the Holy Spirit. The Holy Spirit guided him, strengthened him, and gave him the power to do the amazing things he did. As we live like Jesus, we need to rely on the Holy Spirit too. The first step is remembering the Holy Spirit is a person we can know, love, and trust.

▶ How can you learn more about the Holy Spirit so you can know him better and rely on him more?

27 WHERE IS THE HOLY SPIRIT?

The Holy Spirit lives in all Christians, leading them, guiding them, and helping them.

ROMANS 8:8-11 (OR 8:9)

Some things are either all or nothing. A light is either on or off. There's no in-between. Something is either living or dead. There's no "sorta alive." And a person either has the Holy Spirit or he or she doesn't have the Holy Spirit. This is what we see in Romans 8. There are two kinds of people in the world: those who have trusted in Jesus and have the Holy Spirit and those who haven't and don't. There's no third option.

Now, this doesn't mean the Holy Spirit has nothing to do with people who haven't believed in Jesus. The Holy Spirit is at work in people's hearts showing them their sins and pointing them to the truth about Jesus. We can and should tell others about Jesus, but it's the Holy Spirit who will draw them to trust in Jesus, just like he did for us. But the Holy Spirit doesn't live within a person who hasn't believed in Jesus.

Once we trust in Jesus, though, the Holy Spirit comes to live within us. He is within you fully and always. He is right there to lead you, guide you, and help you. The Holy Spirit will lead you to live for Jesus, guide you to make the right choices each day, and help you when you're in need. His love for you and help for you are limitless! Forgiveness from sin is an amazing gift that God gives us, but then God keeps giving us more and more wonderful gifts, including the Holy Spirit who is always within us.

▶ *What other things can you think of that are all-or-nothing?*

WHERE IS THE HOLY SPIRIT?

▶ How confident are you that the Holy Spirit lives within you?

1 — 2 — 3 — 4 — 5 — 6 — 7 — 8 — 9 — 10

I REALLY DOUBT IT   I'M SURE OF IT

▶ What questions do you have so far?

▶ What are you wondering about because of what you've heard?

PRAYER

God, thank you for giving us the Holy Spirit to live within us and to lead us, guide us, and help us. Amen.

FAMILY ACTIVITY: PLAY

Do it. Play the shell game by hiding an object under one of three identical containers, then shuffling them around to see if anyone can guess where the object is.

Discuss it. Talk about how it can be difficult to tell which container is hiding the object because they all look the same.

Connect it. Share how the Holy Spirit within us doesn't want to be hidden from others. He wants everyone to know he is within us by the way we live.

▼ JESUS CONNECTION ▼

When we think about the Holy Spirit coming to live within us, it reminds us of what Jesus did when he humbly came to earth to live here for a time. But while Jesus left earth and returned to heaven after a while, the Holy Spirit will never leave us. When we humbly follow the Holy Spirit within us, we copy the humility of Jesus.

▶ What can you do to remember that the Holy Spirit is always within you?

28 HOW DOES THE HOLY SPIRIT LEAD US?

The Holy Spirit leads us by showing us ways to love God and people, and by teaching us the best way to live.

LUKE 4:1-13 (OR 4:1-2)

The key to playing follow the leader is paying close attention to the leader and doing exactly what he or she does, whether you want to or not. Sure, you can pay attention to other things and you can do only some of the things the leader does. But you won't win that way. To win, you need to focus on the leader and follow that leader no matter what.

That's what it's like to follow the Holy Spirit. The Holy Spirit leads us each day to find ways to love God, to love other people, and to live the best way. He wants us to follow him so we can please God and enjoy life the way God meant us to enjoy it. But that doesn't mean we'll do these things automatically. We need to pay close attention to the Holy Spirit, listening for him to guide us. Then, we must do what he says. It won't always be easy, but it'll always be worth it. This is what Jesus shows us.

At the start of Jesus' earthly ministry, the Holy Spirit led him into the wilderness, but not for a big celebration or anything like that. Instead, Jesus spent forty days in the wilderness fasting—which means going without food—and being tempted by the devil. There was nothing fun about that! So why did the Holy Spirit lead Jesus there? Because out in that wilderness, Jesus resisted the devil's temptations. And in doing that, Jesus shows us he deserves our love and loyalty. It wasn't easy for Jesus, but in the end, it was all worth it. The Holy Spirit might lead us to do difficult things too, but it will always be worth it.

▶ *If you were the leader of your family, neighborhood, or school, what would you want to do?*

HOW DOES THE HOLY SPIRIT LEAD US?   67

▶ **How do you feel about following the Holy Spirit?**

1 — 2 — 3 — 4 — 5 — 6 — 7 — 8 — 9 — 10

NO WAY!   LET'S DO IT!

▶ **What questions do you have so far?**

▶ **What are you wondering about because of what you've heard?**

PRAYER

God, thank you for giving us the Holy Spirit to lead us every day in whatever we do. Amen.

FAMILY ACTIVITY: PLAY

Do it. Play follow the leader. Start as the leader and make the game easy before gradually making it more difficult.

Discuss it. Talk about the challenges you each faced while playing the game. What makes following a leader hard?

Connect it. Share how following the Holy Spirit might be easy at times and hard at other times, but it's always worth it.

▼ JESUS CONNECTION ▼

Jesus had to trust the Holy Spirit when he followed him into the wilderness. We sometimes think everything was easy for Jesus because he is God, but we can't forget that Jesus became fully human too. That's why going into the wilderness to face the devil wasn't easy for him. As we look to live like Jesus, we need to grow in our trust of the Holy Spirit too.

▶ **How can you grow and increase your trust in the Holy Spirit's leading?**

29

HOW DOES THE HOLY SPIRIT GUIDE US?

The Holy Spirit guides us by showing us the steps to take each day.

ACTS 13:1-3 (OR 13:2)

Have you ever walked across a stream or shallow river? It can be tricky, can't it? Not because of the moving water, but because of the super slippery rocks under that water. What helps is to follow someone who knows exactly where you should place your feet to avoid stepping on those slippery rocks. That person is called a guide. And a guide can make all the difference between successfully crossing a river or falling and floating downstream.

Do you ever wish you had a guide in life? Someone who could show you exactly what to do in any situation? Well, there's great news for you! When you trust in Jesus, you get a guide just like that—the Holy Spirit. The Holy Spirit helps us by showing us what's best to do. He also shows us what *not* to do at times, guiding us away from trouble. And best of all, the Holy Spirit is God, meaning he's not just a good guide; he's a perfect one.

This is what the early church discovered. In Acts 13, the Holy Spirit guided the church at Antioch to send out Barnabas and Paul as missionaries. Most of the rest of the book of Acts describes their missionary journeys and how the church experienced amazing growth because of them. The Holy Spirit didn't guess who to send or what they should do. He knew exactly who was best to go and what was best for them to do. He showed the church, and us, that he truly is the perfect guide!

▶ *Would you rather be a guide, leading travelers on a journey, or a traveler following a guide on a journey?*

► How much do you trust the Holy Spirit to guide you?

1 — 2 — 3 — 4 — 5 — 6 — 7 — 8 — 9 — 10

I'M GOING TO FALL!   I'M GOING TO MAKE IT!

► What questions do you have so far?

► What are you wondering about because of what you've heard?

PRAYER

God, thank you for giving us the Holy Spirit to guide our steps each day. Amen.

FAMILY ACTIVITY: EXPERIMENT

Do it. Go somewhere new or move your furniture around in your home. Take turns blindfolding one person and guiding him or her through the area.

Discuss it. Talk about how it can be difficult to trust a guide, even when you know that person loves you and knows what's best.

Connect it. Share how we can trust the Holy Spirit completely. He's our perfect God who knows everything and loves us fully.

▼ JESUS CONNECTION ▼

When we trust the Holy Spirit and let him guide us where to go and what to do, we follow the example of Jesus. When Jesus was on earth, he let the Spirit guide him too. It wasn't always easy for Jesus, and it won't always be easy for us, but we can always know that the Holy Spirit is our perfect guide.

► How can you listen for the Holy Spirit's guidance today?

30

HOW DOES THE HOLY SPIRIT HELP US?

The Holy Spirit helps us by comforting us when we are worried, afraid, or sad and by convicting us when we sin so we will repent and turn back to God.

JOHN 14:25-27 (OR 14:26-27)

Usually it's wrong to fight, but there's at least one time when it's good to fight: when we fight against sin. Because we like to sin so much, at times we need to fight against our own desires. We won't always win, but if we don't fight, we'll always lose. In time, though, as we fight sin, we'll see more and more wins over it. Although we'll never stop sinning completely, as we continue to fight it, we'll sin less.

The good news is that we aren't alone in this fight. The Holy Spirit is right there with us. He is always with us to convict us of our sin. That means he helps us to know we've sinned and to feel sorry we did. Sometimes we might feel sorry we got caught doing something wrong, but that's not what this is. This isn't about feeling bad about ourselves either, as if we're failures. God always loves us! Instead, this is about the Holy Spirit helping us see that sin is never good for God or ourselves as he increases our desire to turn from sin and turn to God instead. That, then, brings us joy.

That's not all the Spirit does for us, though. He also comforts us and gives us peace, which is what Jesus promised in John 14. God wants us to live with joy, hope, and confidence, but there will be times when we're worried, afraid, or sad or we feel alone, forgotten, or rejected. In those times, the Holy Spirit comforts us and reminds us of God's truth. God is our protector and friend. God values us. He accepts us. And nothing will change that. Whenever you feel down, you can turn to the Holy Spirit for comfort!

▶ **How does it make you feel knowing the Holy Spirit is always with you and wants to comfort you?**

HOW DOES THE HOLY SPIRIT HELP US?

▶ How do you feel about sin?

1 — 2 — 3 — 4 — 5 — 6 — 7 — 8 — 9 — 10
I LOVE IT   I CAN'T STAND IT

▶ What questions do you have so far?

▶ What are you wondering about because of what you've heard?

PRAYER

God, thank you for comforting us through the Holy Spirit, especially when life is difficult. Amen.

FAMILY ACTIVITY: EXPERIMENT

Do it. Go to a bedding store and determine the most comfortable bed and pillows.

Discuss it. Talk about how there are many kinds of beds and pillows, and everyone tends to have a different idea of what's most comfortable.

Connect it. Share how the soft, comfortable beds can't even come close to the comfort the Holy Spirit gives us.

▼ JESUS CONNECTION ▼

The Holy Spirit comforting us reminds us of God's wonderful compassion for us. God loves us and cares deeply for us. This is how Jesus lived on earth. He had deep compassion for people, even when it wasn't convenient for him to act on that compassion. As we grow to live more like Jesus, loving others and having compassion for them is an important part of what we can do.

▶ How can you show compassion for others and care for them this week?

31

WHAT IS THE FRUIT OF THE SPIRIT?

The fruit of the Spirit is love, joy, peace, patience, kindness, goodness, faithfulness, gentleness, and self-control.

GALATIANS 5:22-23

You might not know much about trees, but you can probably recognize an apple tree when you see one—if it has apples on it. The same is true of an orange tree, a cherry tree, a pear tree, or a peach tree. You might not know these trees by their shape, bark, or leaves, but if one has fruit on it, you have a good chance of telling what it is. Why? Because apple trees produce apples, orange trees produce oranges, and peach trees produce peaches; it's just what they do. And that's how they're recognized.

Did you know that people should be able to tell we've trusted in Jesus the same way we can recognize fruit trees? That's right, people should see our fruit and recognize that we belong to Jesus. We're not talking about apples or oranges, but rather the fruit of the Spirit—love, joy, peace, patience, kindness, goodness, faithfulness, gentleness, and self-control. When people see us, they should see this fruit, and when they see this fruit, they'll know there's something different about us. They'll recognize that we look a lot like Jesus!

But don't miss something important: this fruit is called the fruit of the Spirit, not the fruit of the believer. We don't produce this fruit; the Holy Spirit does. He works in us and through us to bring these wonderful characteristics out of us. While people who haven't trusted in Jesus can also show these traits, only when we've trusted in Jesus can we show them to the amazing degree that can make people stop and notice. And when they do—when someone asks how we can be so kind or patient—our answer should always be the same: it's not me, it's the Holy Spirit working in me!

▶ *What is your favorite fruit?*

WHAT IS THE FRUIT OF THE SPIRIT? 73

▶ **What sort of fruit can others usually see in you?**

1 — 2 — 3 — 4 — 5 — 6 — 7 — 8 — 9 — 10
SOUR AND BITTER   SWEET AND PLEASANT

▶ **What questions do you have so far?**

▶ **What are you wondering about because of what you've heard?**

PRAYER

God, thank you for producing the fruit of the Spirit in us. Amen.

FAMILY ACTIVITY: EXPERIMENT

Do it. Visit the produce section of a grocery store and purchase as many different types of fruit as you can.

Discuss it. As you sample the fruits, talk about their different colors, flavors, smells, and textures. Determine which you like the most and why.

Connect it. Share how we bring the "flavor" of Jesus to the world when the Holy Spirit produces his fruit in us.

▼ JESUS CONNECTION ▼

One of the amazing things about Jesus is that people were drawn to him. They just couldn't get enough of him! That's because it was clear Jesus loved people and cared for them—he demonstrated the fruit of the Spirit. As we let the Spirit work in and through us, we will live just like Jesus with the hope that we too can be used to help change people's lives.

▶ **What are some ways you can show the fruit of the Spirit to others this week?**

32

HOW CAN WE DISPLAY THE FRUIT OF THE SPIRIT?

We can display the fruit of the Spirit by living by the Holy Spirit.

GALATIANS 5:24-26 (OR 5:25)

Apple trees naturally produce apples, but they don't automatically produce apples. God made apple trees to produce crisp, sweet apples, but apple trees can't do that if they don't get the water and nutrients they need. That means if you owned an apple orchard, you couldn't just sit in a rocking chair all day waiting to pick apples. You'd need to spend quite a bit of time and energy taking care of your apple trees so they could produce the best apples possible. The same is true for the fruit of the Spirit.

At times, anyone can display some amount of love, joy, peace, patience, kindness, goodness, faithfulness, gentleness, and self-control. But only a believer, within whom the Holy Spirit has produced this fruit, can show these qualities as fully and wonderfully as God intends. Anyone can be loving for a moment, especially when it's convenient and the other person is lovable. But as followers of Jesus, we can go beyond that and love the unlovable even when it's inconvenient.

This is why Galatians 5:25 tells us that we must live by the Holy Spirit. This means we are to follow the Holy Spirit's leading and guidance as we let him grow us and shape us to become the kind of person who looks like Jesus. When we do this—when we follow the Holy Spirit instead of ourselves—he will do amazing things through us that we could never do on our own! Just like apple trees need to be healthy to make apples, we need to be "healthy" too. And the best way for us to be healthy is to live by the Holy Spirit and trust him to change us, use us, and produce the sweetest fruit through us.

▶ *If you could grow any food on a tree, what would it be?*

HOW CAN WE DISPLAY THE FRUIT OF THE SPIRIT?

▶ How healthy are you for the Holy Spirit to produce his fruit in you?

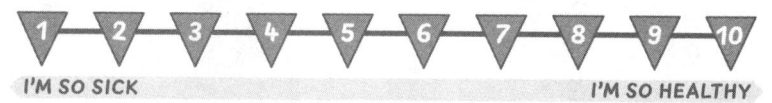

1 — 2 — 3 — 4 — 5 — 6 — 7 — 8 — 9 — 10

I'M SO SICK   I'M SO HEALTHY

▶ What questions do you have so far?

▶ What are you wondering about because of what you've heard?

PRAYER

God, thank you for giving us the Holy Spirit to lead us, guide us, and change us so we can experience the best life possible. Amen.

FAMILY ACTIVITY: CREATE

Do it. Plant a fruit tree or bush or a seed for a fruit-bearing tree or bush.

Discuss it. As you put the seed, tree, or bush in the ground and water and fertilize it, talk about what it will need to grow and be healthy and how long it might take before you can eat its fruit.

Connect it. Share ways we can prepare ourselves (e.g., Bible reading, praying) for the Holy Spirit to produce fruit in and through us.

▼ JESUS CONNECTION ▼

Living by the Holy Spirit isn't easy. It takes humility. Jesus gives us a great picture of this humility. Jesus is fully God, but while he was here on earth he lived by the Holy Spirit and followed his guidance. That took great humility on Jesus' part, but he did it without any hesitation and with complete trust and joy. And so can we.

▶ How can you humbly live by the Holy Spirit today?

33

HOW CAN WE LIVE BY THE HOLY SPIRIT?

We can live by the Holy Spirit by being filled by him moment by moment.

ACTS 2:1-5, 22-24 (OR 2:4-5)

Have you played a video game where you controlled a character on the screen? When you wanted it to go left, it went left. When you wanted it to go right, it went right. When you wanted it to jump, run, or do anything else, it would do it. That character did only what you wanted it to do.

That's a picture of what it means to live by the Holy Spirit. When we live by the Spirit, we give control of our lives to him. We listen to him closely and carefully and follow him however and wherever he guides us. Very simply, we do what the Spirit wants. The Bible calls this being "filled by the Spirit" (Ephesians 5:18).

Imagine you had a cup and some milk and orange juice. If you filled the cup with milk there would be no room for the orange juice. That's what we are to do with the Holy Spirit. We're to allow him to fill us completely so there's no room for anything else to guide us. When that happens, the Holy Spirit will produce his fruit in us and guide us to live like Jesus! This is what we see happen in Acts 2, when the disciples were filled with the Holy Spirit and they powerfully shared about Jesus.

Even so, it can be hard to give up control of our lives and live by the Holy Spirit. But don't forget what we get when we do: love, joy, peace, patience, kindness, goodness, faithfulness, gentleness, and self-control. Don't you want as much of the fruit of the Spirit as possible? To experience this fruit, we must trust God and remember that his ways and plans are always so much better than ours.

▶ *If you could fill a swimming pool with any kind of candy you wanted, what would it be?*

HOW CAN WE LIVE BY THE HOLY SPIRIT?

▶ How do you feel about giving control of your life to the Holy Spirit?

1 — 2 — 3 — 4 — 5 — 6 — 7 — 8 — 9 — 10
IT'S REALLY SCARY — IT'S REALLY EXCITING

▶ What questions do you have so far?

▶ What are you wondering about because of what you've heard?

PRAYER

God, thank you that when we live by the Holy Spirit, we will never be disappointed and we will always do what is best. Amen.

FAMILY ACTIVITY: COMPETE

Do it. Take turns pouring water into a container. Each person can pour as much water as he or she wants, but something must be poured in. The person who makes the container overflow is out. Play additional rounds to determine a champion.

Discuss it. As you play, talk about how the container can look filled when it really isn't. As long as there's even a tiny amount of room, it's not full.

Connect it. Share how life works best when we are completely filled by the Holy Spirit.

▼ JESUS CONNECTION ▼

The key to living by the Spirit just might be love. We need to love the Holy Spirit enough to want him to fill us, and we need to love other people enough to want to follow the Holy Spirit no matter what. This is what Jesus did. He did everything out of love. When we love the Father and others like Jesus does, we'll be controlled by the Holy Spirit to live more like Jesus.

▶ How can you grow in your love for God and other people this week?

PART 4

PEOPLE AND SIN

WHAT THE BIBLE TEACHES ABOUT PEOPLE, a field of study called *anthropology*, is a little complicated. On one hand, people are recognized as the pinnacle of creation (Psalm 8:4-6), bearers of God's image (Genesis 1:26), and of exceeding worth (Psalm 139:13-16). But on the other hand, people are sinners in rebellion against a good and holy God (Romans 5:6-10), deserving of eternal condemnation. Some places in Scripture even liken us to a lowly maggot or worm (Job 25:6; Psalm 22:6).

So what are we to pass along to our children about who they are? Are they wonderful or terrible? Well, both. Humans are simply wonderfully terrible and terribly wonderful! The key is understanding that this might seem like a contradiction, but it's not. These two critical concepts complement each other.

The first two questions in this section begin with the positive—our value before God and the reason we exist. One of the more important things we can do for our children is help secure a proper positive self-worth within them, a self-image based on their unchanging identity given by God and the never-changing fact that God's love is fixed on them. This will be the strong, sure foundation they can build their lives on, a foundation that can weather any storm in life, even the most intense one. Thinking poorly of ourselves isn't humility; it's failing to appreciate and agree with God's perspective of who we are. May our kids never doubt their infinite worth as humans loved by God and made in his image for a special purpose!

At the same time, as we see what the Bible teaches about sin (an area of theology called *hamartiology*), we can't help but appreciate how far we fall short of our design and purpose. We can't dismiss how sin has completely and totally corrupted us in every way, severing our relationship with God. This is essential to understanding the gospel. Just as the brightest fireworks require the darkest night behind them to display their brilliance, so too does the dark backdrop of sin reveal the beauty of the gospel.

We need to be careful not to hold these truths out of balance. Focusing too much on our design while minimizing sin results in a watered-down gospel. It leads to thinking and living as if we are good with God when that isn't true apart from Jesus. Focusing too much on our sin while minimizing our design results in a neglected gospel. It leads to legalistic, graceless, joyless thinking and living as if we are never good with God, even when we have Jesus. Indeed, the gospel needs both. The work of Jesus is to overcome sin and restore marvelous people back to their right and fitting place in God's creation.

34

WHO WERE THE FIRST PEOPLE GOD CREATED?

God created Adam as the first man and Eve as the first woman.

GENESIS 2:5-7, 18-23 (OR 2:7, 18)

God created everything that exists except for himself. The earth, sun, moon, stars, planets, mountains, oceans, and animals—God created it all. Everything God created is amazing, and it all shows how God as its Creator is even more amazing. But of all the many wonderful things God made, one thing in particular stands out as the absolute best of the best: people. Everything God made is magnificent, but he made us most magnificent of all.

God loves everything he made, but he loves us more than anything else. Everything God made is special, but he made us most special of all. And it all began with one man and one woman: Adam and Eve. From this one couple all other people came into being. That means we're all really one huge family!

Genesis 2 tells us God made Adam first, out of the ground, and then God made Eve, from part of Adam. Some people think it was Adam's rib, but it could have been part of his side (Genesis 2:21). No matter how God made Adam and Eve, what's clear is that he made them for a purpose: to know him and have a friendship with him. But that wasn't all. He also made people to be friends with one another. Our relationship with God matters most of all, but our relationship with other people is a close second. We weren't made to live in a bubble; we were made to live in a community. God has given us a wonderful gift in being able to know him, but he has also given us an amazing gift in having family and friends.

▶ *Who are some of your best friends?*

WHO WERE THE FIRST PEOPLE GOD CREATED?

▶ How important are your friends to you?

1 — 2 — 3 — 4 — 5 — 6 — 7 — 8 — 9 — 10

THEY'RE PRETTY OKAY   THEY'RE PRETTY AMAZING

▶ What questions do you have so far?

▶ What are you wondering about because of what you've heard?

PRAYER

God, thank you for making people, including us, the most special part of your creation. Amen.

FAMILY ACTIVITY: EXPLORE

Do it. Pick a new activity or restaurant to try.

Discuss it. Talk about what you liked or didn't like about the experience and whether trying new things tends to be more fun or more scary.

Connect it. Share how everything Adam and Eve experienced was new for them and how curious they must have been about it all.

▼ JESUS CONNECTION ▼

It's important to recognize how special you are to God, but at the same time, it's important to be humble. Jesus shows us just how this balance works. When Jesus was on earth, he never thought lowly of himself, but he didn't refuse to lower himself to serve others either. This is how we are to live, never thinking for a minute that we don't matter while we treat others like they matter even more.

▶ How can you humbly serve others this week?

35 WHY DID GOD CREATE ADAM AND EVE?

God created Adam and Eve, perfect and innocent, to know him, love him, worship him, and obey him.

1 CORINTHIANS 10:31

A hammer is a wonderful tool for driving nails into wood, but it's a terrible tool for eating breakfast cereal. The reason is pretty obvious: a hammer isn't meant to be a spoon any more than a spoon is meant to be a hammer. Everything works best when it's used according to its design and for its intended purpose. That includes people.

Have you ever wondered why God made people? We find the answer starting with Adam and Eve. In Genesis 1–2, we see that God made Adam and Eve perfect and innocent so they could know him, our perfect and holy God. And when you know God, it's quite difficult not to love him and worship him!

But God also gave Adam and Eve an assignment—something they were to do. They were to take care of God's creation and start a family. So in addition to knowing, loving, and worshiping God, Adam and Eve were to obey God. And we are to do all that too.

Paul summed this up in 1 Corinthians 10:31 when he said whatever we do, we are to do it to glorify God. To glorify God is to celebrate him. It's to enjoy him and to point others to how amazing he is. That's our one, big, important job. Sometimes it's easy to know how to glorify God; at other times it can be challenging. The Bible doesn't tell us exactly what to do in every situation. But that's one reason why he has given us the Holy Spirit. The Spirit points us to the best way we can live to look like Jesus and to glorify God in all we do.

▶ *Would you rather eat with only a hammer for the rest of your life or build a house with only a spoon?*

WHY DID GOD CREATE ADAM AND EVE?

▶ How much do you understand what it means to glorify God?

1 — 2 — 3 — 4 — 5 — 6 — 7 — 8 — 9 — 10

I'M SO LOST   I'VE GOT THIS

▶ What questions do you have so far?

▶ What are you wondering about because of what you've heard?

PRAYER

God, thank you for giving us such an amazing purpose to know you, love you, worship you, and obey you. Amen.

FAMILY ACTIVITY: CREATE

Do it. Try to make a craft, build an item, or play a game without any equipment or with the wrong equipment.

Discuss it. Talk about how difficult and perhaps frustrating this experience was.

Connect it. Share how the same thing often happens when we don't live out our purpose of glorifying God.

▼ JESUS CONNECTION ▼

Sometimes it's hard to stay focused on our wonderful purpose of glorifying God. There are so many things to distract us! Jesus had tons of distractions too, but he remembered that the Father is most important of all, so he lived every day to celebrate him. We can do the same. Start by focusing on God today. Then tomorrow. Then this week. Then this month. Then this year. Eventually it will turn into a lifetime!

▶ *How will you focus on God and spend time with him today?*

36 DID ADAM AND EVE REMAIN PERFECT AND INNOCENT?

No. Adam and Eve disobeyed God, and from that moment on, they were no longer perfect and innocent.

GENESIS 3:6-13 (OR 3:6-7)

God placed Adam and Eve in the Garden of Eden with everything they needed. They had a perfect relationship with God and a perfect relationship with one another. They had all the food they could ever want. They never got sick, they never got lonely or sad, and they would never die. All they had to do was obey God's one simple command not to eat the fruit of the tree of the knowledge of good and evil.

But they couldn't do that. Instead, they chose to disobey their loving and good Creator. Tragically, everything fell apart.

We don't know how much time took place between God making Adam and Eve in Genesis 2 and Adam and Eve making the terrible choice to disobey God in Genesis 3. It could have been days, weeks, months, years, decades, or even longer. But no matter how long it was, it only took a split second—the snap of a finger—for everything to break. The instant Adam and Eve disobeyed God and ate the fruit of the forbidden tree, they went from being perfect to being sinful and they went from being innocent to being guilty. Snap! Just like that.

This is what sin does: it promises to give us so much, but in reality, it takes everything away from us. From that day on, people have been trying to make the huge jump back from Genesis 3 to Genesis 2—to go from brokenness back to perfection. But it's a leap backward that no one can make, at least not on our own. Thankfully, God provided the one and only way for us to become perfect and innocent once again. His name is Jesus!

▶ *What do you think life was like for Adam and Eve before they disobeyed God in Genesis 3?*

DID ADAM AND EVE REMAIN PERFECT AND INNOCENT? 85

▶ How far from perfect and innocent do you think you are?

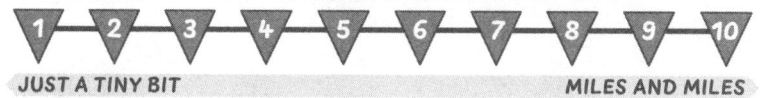

1 — 2 — 3 — 4 — 5 — 6 — 7 — 8 — 9 — 10
JUST A TINY BIT   MILES AND MILES

▶ What questions do you have so far?

▶ What are you wondering about because of what you've heard?

PRAYER

God, thank you for forgiving us of our sins through Jesus and for giving us the Holy Spirit to help us stand against sin. Amen.

FAMILY ACTIVITY: PLAY

Do it. Play or watch a sport.

Discuss it. Talk about how highly trained, skilled, experienced athletes often fail at their sport. In baseball, for example, the best batters fail about seventy percent of the time!

Connect it. Share how it's impossible for us to obey God perfectly, but he has forgiven us through Jesus and given us the Holy Spirit to help us stand strong.

▼ JESUS CONNECTION ▼

When the devil tempted Adam and Eve, they gave in and sinned. But when the devil tempted Jesus, he didn't give in or sin. Jesus shows us that when we trust in God and rely on his strength, we don't have to sin. The key is not to rely on our own strength but on the strength we've been given by the Holy Spirit who lives within us!

▶ How can you trust in the Holy Spirit's strength when you are tempted to disobey God?

37 WHY DID ADAM AND EVE DISOBEY GOD?

Because Eve wanted to be like God, she ate the forbidden fruit, and so did Adam who was with her.

GENESIS 3:1-6 (OR 3:4-5)

God was clear. If Adam and Eve disobeyed and ate from the forbidden tree, they would die. Not that they *might* die. Or even that they'd *probably* die. God said they *would* die.

But one day, the devil used the serpent to mislead Eve. Some people think the devil looked like a serpent; others think he used a serpent. Either way, we know that the devil was ultimately the one behind tricking Eve and getting her and Adam to disobey God's command.

The serpent used half-truths and total lies to cause Eve to doubt God. He got Eve to believe that God was withholding something good from her and Adam rather than protecting them from something very bad. The serpent confused Eve into believing she deserved more than what God was providing. When the serpent got her to that point, he told her what she really "needed." If she ate from the forbidden tree—even if that meant disobeying God—she wouldn't die but would become like God.

This, of course, was a lie. But Eve believed the lie, and Adam, who was with her, did too. What they thought would make them equal with God drove them as far away from him as possible.

We disobey God for the same reason. Each time we sin it's because we want to have the final say over our lives. We want to be in control. We want to be God. And just like with Adam and Eve, our sins never give us what we hope for. Instead, they always lead us right where sin led Adam and Eve: straight into trouble. It's a good thing sin doesn't have the final say in our lives—Jesus does!

▶ **What are some things that tempt you the most?**

▶ **If God had created you first, do you think you would have eaten the forbidden fruit?**

1 — 2 — 3 — 4 — 5 — 6 — 7 — 8 — 9 — 10

NEVER!   IMMEDIATELY!

▶ What questions do you have so far?

▶ What are you wondering about because of what you've heard?

PRAYER

God, thank you for forgiving us through Jesus and helping us say no to sin through his truth and the Holy Spirit's help. Amen.

FAMILY ACTIVITY: EXPERIMENT

Do it. Go to a fast-food restaurant and compare what your food looks like with the pictures on the menu.

Discuss it. Talk about how and why restaurants "stretch" the truth at times to make the food look better than it usually is in real life.

Connect it. Share how this is what the devil did in Eden and what he still tries to do today.

▼ JESUS CONNECTION ▼

The problem began when Adam and Eve got confused about God's truth. That can happen to us too, and it's just as dangerous. But we don't have to be confused! Jesus said he is the truth (John 14:6). This means everything he said and did is true. All we need to do, then, is look toward Jesus. Jesus helps us know truth and helps us live in truth too.

▶ *What truths can you remember to help you say no to sin, along with the Holy Spirit's help?*

38

WHAT HAPPENED TO ADAM AND EVE WHEN THEY DISOBEYED GOD?

The moment Adam and Eve disobeyed God they became sinful and separated from God.

ROMANS 6:23

God warned Adam and Eve that if they ate the forbidden fruit, they would die. The serpent, however, said that wasn't true. He said that if Adam and Eve ate the fruit, they wouldn't die. Guess who was right? God was. God's warning came true in two different ways.

First, after Adam and Eve ate the fruit, instead of being glad to see God and rushing toward him when he came into the garden, they were ashamed of what they had done and hid themselves. Of all the terrible consequences of sin, this one is by far the worst. God had made Adam and Eve to be with him—to be close to him and to love and enjoy him. But because of their disobedience, Adam and Eve ran from God. They were afraid of him and didn't want to see him. It was completely backward!

Our sin does the same thing. Because of our sins, we too are separated from our holy God. This is what Romans 6:23 tells us. Because of our sin, we've earned death, which is sometimes called spiritual death. We're separated from God and unable to live forever with him.

Second, even though it didn't happen right away, Adam and Eve also died physically. They grew quite old (Adam lived 930 years; Genesis 5:5), but at some point, they experienced exactly what God had promised. God is always truthful, even when that truth is difficult.

God didn't design us to die, spiritually or physically. He made us to live forever with him. We can't fix what we broke, but our amazing God can and that's what he did! Because of Jesus, we can have back what we lost. When we trust in Jesus, we might still die physically, but we will live with God forever.

▶ *Have you ever been separated and lost? How did it feel?*

WHAT HAPPENED TO ADAM AND EVE?

▶ How excited are you about living with God forever?

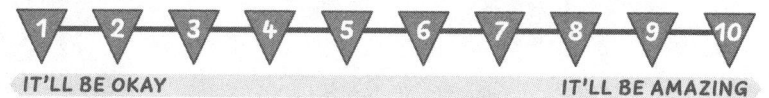

1 — 2 — 3 — 4 — 5 — 6 — 7 — 8 — 9 — 10

IT'LL BE OKAY   IT'LL BE AMAZING

▶ What questions do you have so far?

▶ What are you wondering about because of what you've heard?

PRAYER

God, thank you for being trustworthy when you warned us about sin and when you promised you'd make a way to forgive us. Amen.

FAMILY ACTIVITY: PLAY

Do it. Play hide-and-seek.

Discuss it. Talk about the challenges of the game and the strategies that can help you win as either the one hiding or the one seeking.

Connect it. Share how the ones hiding in the game are a picture of what sin has done—it has separated us from God. Then share how the one seeking is like Jesus. Jesus came to seek us and save us!

▼ JESUS CONNECTION ▼

We don't deserve God the Father's forgiveness, but because of his great love for us, he's given it to us through Jesus. No amount of sin is too large and no sin is too terrible for God's forgiveness. Jesus gave up his life for all of it. That's how God wants us to live too. We can't give up our lives to forgive sin, but we can be willing to forgive others when they wrong us.

▶ What will you do the next time someone does something wrong to you?

39

WHAT PROMISE DID GOD MAKE TO ADAM AND EVE AFTER THEY SINNED?

God promised Adam and Eve that one of their offspring, Jesus, would be the Rescuer to strike the head of the serpent and bring victory.

GENESIS 3:14-15

Can we be honest? Some of the Bible isn't very fun to read, is it? Parts can be tough. Sometimes the Bible can be discouraging and frustrating. Sometimes it can even be a little scary. Genesis 3 is like that. If only Adam and Eve had just listened to God and refused to eat from that one tree! But they ate. And because they ate, we're in quite a mess. The entire world is broken, and that includes us. But we shouldn't be too hard on Adam and Eve. We wouldn't have done any better in Eden. We would have broken everything too.

As dark as this chapter is, it isn't dark enough to overcome a brilliant light of hope we can see right in the middle of it all. When God judges the serpent, he tells it that he will put hostility between the serpent's offspring and Eve's offspring—someone born into her family one day. The serpent will strike the heel of Eve's offspring while her offspring will strike the serpent's head.

Is this God's way of saying people wouldn't like snakes? Not at all! This is the Bible's first prophecy about Jesus. Jesus would be Eve's offspring who would be struck by the devil. That happened on the cross. But that strike wouldn't be final. Jesus would die, but he wouldn't stay dead. On the third day, Jesus rose from the dead, and that became the devil's fatal blow. This verse is all about the cross and the empty tomb!

Even in the middle of God judging Adam and Eve for their rebellion, he provides this wonderful and beautiful picture of the grace and victory we receive through Jesus. God sure is wonderful, isn't he?

▶ How do you feel about snakes?

WHAT PROMISE DID GOD MAKE TO ADAM AND EVE?

▶ How sure are you that Jesus has rescued you from sin and death?

1 — 2 — 3 — 4 — 5 — 6 — 7 — 8 — 9 — 10

I'VE GOT MY DOUBTS   NO QUESTION ABOUT IT

▶ What questions do you have so far?

▶ What are you wondering about because of what you've heard?

PRAYER

God, thank you for loving us and for Jesus dying on the cross and coming back to life again so we can be forgiven. Amen.

FAMILY ACTIVITY: PLAY

Do it. Watch or participate in a sporting event.

Discuss it. Talk about how sometimes a win can be snatched from defeat at the last minute. Gloom and despair can turn into joy and celebration in an instant.

Connect it. Share how that's what God did for us through the cross and the empty tomb. Just when all seemed lost, Jesus rose back to life and defeated sin and death!

▼ JESUS CONNECTION ▼

What the devil thought was his victory—the cross—was actually his defeat. It's only through Jesus' sacrifice and death on the cross that we can have life. We can't live like Jesus by giving up our lives to provide forgiveness for others, but we can sacrifice for others. In big ways and in small ways, when we live in humility and sacrifice for someone else's good, we act like Jesus!

▶ *What can you sacrifice for someone this week?*

40

HOW DOES ADAM AND EVE'S SIN AFFECT PEOPLE?

Because of Adam and Eve's sin, all people since have been born with a sin nature.

ROMANS 5:12

Do you remember who taught you how to lie? How did you learn to be jealous of your friends for having something you didn't have? Who taught you how to be angry? You can't remember, can you? That's because no one taught you these things. And that's because no one needed to. All these sinful actions came naturally for you because they come naturally for all of us. We are sinners by nature. That means no one has to teach us how to sin. It comes as natural to us as breathing. But this isn't the way it's always been.

When God made Adam and Eve, they were pure and innocent. But once they ate the forbidden fruit and sin entered the world, everyone since then has been born with a nature to sin. That's what Paul tells us in Romans 5:12. Our natural tendency is now to rebel against God instead of following him. We might not rebel in huge, obvious ways. But we surely do in small ways at least. Since Adam and Eve, every single person who has been born—except for Jesus—has been born a sinner. And because of this, we're all under God's judgment of sin.

The world wants to believe that people are basically good. Without a doubt, we are still the most special part of creation and God still loves us more than we can imagine. But because of sin, we are nowhere near as good as we can and should be. In fact, we are much more likely to disobey God and do wrong things instead of good things. Apple trees produce apples because they're apple trees. People sin because we're sinners. But Jesus came to change that!

▶ *What are some things people do naturally without needing to be taught?*

HOW DOES ADAM AND EVE'S SIN AFFECT PEOPLE?

▶ How good are you at sinning?

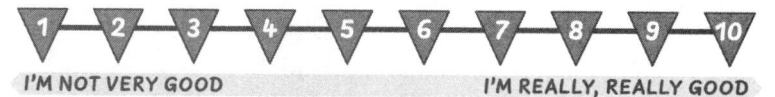

1 — 2 — 3 — 4 — 5 — 6 — 7 — 8 — 9 — 10

I'M NOT VERY GOOD   I'M REALLY, REALLY GOOD

▶ What questions do you have so far?

▶ What are you wondering about because of what you've heard?

PRAYER

God, thank you for providing Jesus as the one and only solution for our sins. Amen.

FAMILY ACTIVITY: OBSERVE

Do it. Search the internet for instructions on how to whistle by using your fingers or how to do some other uncommon skill.

Discuss it. As you learn the skill, talk about the need for patience and practice.

Connect it. Share how sin isn't learned, but rather it comes easily for us. We're all instantly good at sinning! But then celebrate how God has provided forgiveness for our sin through Jesus and all we have to do is trust in him.

▼ JESUS CONNECTION ▼

Every single person Jesus knew and loved while he was on earth sinned, and each of their sins—and ours—is what led Jesus to the cross. Even still, Jesus loved each of those people and he loves us. Jesus doesn't love our sins, of course. But he loves us despite our sins. We can do the same. We shouldn't accept sin, but we should always love others, no matter what sins they do.

▶ How can you grow in your love for others, despite how they might sin?

41

WHAT IS SIN?

Sin is disobeying God by doing what he forbids, not doing what he commands, or not having the right attitude toward him or others.

2 TIMOTHY 3:1-5 (OR 3:2-4)

Have you ever watched or been in an archery competition? You can probably picture the target in your mind right now: a large circle with several smaller circles evenly spaced inside it. Think about the smallest circle in the very center of the target—the bull's-eye. This is what you aim for, right? Your goal is to hit this circle, not the other ones. If you hit this inside circle, you've had a good shot. But if you hit anything else, you've missed. That's really what those other circles measure: how much you missed the bull's-eye.

This might help you understand sin. The Bible teaches that our target—the bull's-eye of all we do—is obeying God. If we do anything besides that, we miss the target and that's called sin. There are places in the Bible that list different sins, like in 2 Timothy 3, but we must be careful not to think what we read there is the only kind of sin. Sin is broader than that. If we don't do what God has told us to do, we miss the target; we sin. If we do what God has told us not to do, we miss the target; we sin. If we don't have the right attitude even while doing the right thing—say, we're obeying our parents by taking out the trash but we're grumpy about it—we miss the target; we sin.

It doesn't matter how close we get to the target. If we don't hit it—even missing it by the smallest amount—we sin. And any one of those sins—even one that was so, so close to hitting the target—is enough to earn God's judgment. That's the bad news. But the great news is that no sin is beyond God's forgiveness through Jesus!

▶ *If you were in an archery competition, how many bull's-eyes do you think you could hit in a row?*

WHAT IS SIN?

▶ **How well do you usually obey God?**

1 — 2 — 3 — 4 — 5 — 6 — 7 — 8 — 9 — 10

I MISS THE TARGET COMPLETELY   I NAIL THAT BULL'S-EYE

▶ **What questions do you have so far?**

▶ **What are you wondering about because of what you've heard?**

PRAYER

God, thank you for Jesus who never sinned and made the one way for us to be forgiven of our sins. Amen.

FAMILY ACTIVITY: COMPETE

Do it. Participate in an archery, axe throwing, or darts outing, or aim at a target with a Nerf toy, rubber bands, or something else at home. Keep track of how many times everyone hits the bull's-eye compared to how many times everyone misses.

Discuss it. Talk about the challenges of hitting the target.

Connect it. Share how anytime we don't obey God fully we miss the bull's-eye.

▼ JESUS CONNECTION ▼

How do we obey God when it's hard or when we really don't want to? The key is love. We need to love God more than anything else and want to please him more than we please ourselves. This is how Jesus lived on earth, and it's how he obeyed the Father. Our obedience comes the same way. Grow in your love for God and your obedience will follow.

▶ *What can you do the next time it's hard to obey God or when you don't feel like it?*

42

WHERE DOES SIN BEGIN?

Sin begins in the heart where we choose not to fulfill our created purpose to know, love, worship, and obey God.

JAMES 1:13-14 (OR 1:14)

When Adam and Eve sinned, God asked them what had happened and they told him something quite interesting. Adam blamed Eve (Genesis 3:12) and Eve blamed the serpent (Genesis 3:13). Neither could own up to the wrong they had done. Instead, they found it easier to blame others.

We can do that too. Sure, there are times when someone helps us sin, like when a friend asks you to help cheat on a test. And the devil and his demons are real, and they do all they can to help us disobey God. But the truth is that we're really, really, really good at sinning on our own. We don't need much help—if any. Remember, we are sinners by nature. That's why we're so good at it. It's just what we do.

The truth is that most often we sin because we want to sin. It can be so appealing! Sin whispers in our ears that it's the path to getting what we want and being happy. And so even if we know better, deep within our hearts we often want to say yes to sin, and that's just what we do. That's what we read about in James 1:14. The greatest danger isn't outside of us; it's within us. Adam and Eve didn't begin to sin when they bit into the fruit or even when they reached out and took hold of it. They began to sin in their hearts when they failed to trust God and when they felt they deserved more from him.

Ultimately, sin isn't a behavior issue; it's a heart issue. It's when our hearts decide they don't want to follow God's ways but rather go their own ways. Thankfully, there's a wonderful cure for this. His name is Jesus!

▶ *What are some good things you're good at?*

WHERE DOES SIN BEGIN?

▶ Who do you tend to blame for your sins?

1—2—3—4—5—6—7—8—9—10

ALWAYS SOMEONE ELSE · ALWAYS ME

▶ What questions do you have so far?

▶ What are you wondering about because of what you've heard?

PRAYER

God, thank you for giving us a wonderful purpose in life and for forgiving us when we forget it or resist it. Amen.

FAMILY ACTIVITY: EXPERIMENT

Do it. Bake a batch of cupcakes, but add some unpleasant ingredients, like tuna, to a few. See who is daring enough to try a bad cupcake.

Discuss it. As you enjoy the good cupcakes, talk about how the quality of a cupcake is based on its ingredients—what's within it.

Connect it. Share how the same is true of people; what is within us determines the most about us.

▼ JESUS CONNECTION ▼

When Jesus came to earth, he had a big purpose of laying down his life for us. He knew this purpose, and he had opportunities to avoid it, but he didn't. Instead, the Father's purpose mattered most to him. Obeying God isn't always easy for us and sometimes disobeying him seems fun. But like Jesus, we need our purpose of knowing, loving, worshiping, and obeying God to matter most.

▶ What can you do this week to remember your God-given purpose?

43

IS THERE ANYONE WHO DOES NOT SIN?

No. Everyone except Jesus sins and is separated from holy God.

ROMANS 3:20-23 (OR 3:23)

Almost everyone is good at dividing people. We love finding ways we're different from each other. That's why we make groups of "us" and "them." What we look like, where we live, how old we are, what language we speak, how much money we have, what our favorite sport or sports team is, what school we go to, and even what kind of phone we use. Sometimes dividing people like this is harmless, but at other times it leads to deep, hurtful sins like racism.

It's true that people are different, but Romans 3:23 teaches us there's one way every single person is exactly alike—there's only one giant group of "us" and there's no "them." That way is sin. We're all sinners. Every single person in all the groups we like to create is a sinner. Think about the meanest, rudest, nastiest person you know. That person is obviously a sinner. But now think of the nicest, kindest, gentlest person you know. That person is a sinner too. And so are we.

Everyone is born with a sin nature and we all do many, many sins out of that sin nature. Everyone, that is, except Jesus. Jesus never sinned. He lived a perfect life. He then died and was raised from the dead so that anyone who believes in him is forgiven of their sins. In this way, Jesus has indeed formed a new group: the forgiven! We are all either unforgiven sinners or sinners who have been forgiven through faith in Jesus. Aren't you grateful for what Jesus has done for us?

▶ *What groups of people can you think of, and which are you part of?*

IS THERE ANYONE WHO DOES NOT SIN?

▶ How do you feel about every single person deserving to be separated from God?

1 — 2 — 3 — 4 — 5 — 6 — 7 — 8 — 9 — 10

IT BOTHERS ME — I AGREE WITH IT

▶ What questions do you have so far?

▶ What are you wondering about because of what you've heard?

PRAYER

God, thank you for making a new group of people who have been forgiven because of Jesus. Amen.

FAMILY ACTIVITY: VISIT

Do it. Attend the symphony or watch an orchestra performance online.

Discuss it. Talk about how the instruments are grouped by type, but they're all part of one symphony and they must work together to make wonderful music.

Connect it. Share how we tend to divide people into groups, like the instrument types, but God sees us all together—as people he loves and wants to forgive and be in a relationship with.

▼ JESUS CONNECTION ▼

One of the many wonderful things about Jesus is he was friends with everyone. He even loved and accepted people who were shunned by others and considered unlovable. That's how we've been called to live too. We're to be like Jesus and refuse to allow the groups the world creates to prevent us from loving others. No one should be beyond our friendship.

▶ How can you be kind, loving, and friendly toward others this week?

44

DO CHRISTIANS SIN?

Yes. Christians continue to sin, although all our sin is forgiven and we have the Holy Spirit to help us resist sin.

1 JOHN 1:5-10 (OR 1:10)

It would be wonderful if we didn't sin after trusting in Jesus. But sadly, that's not the case. Even though we're made new in Jesus, we still sin. That's what 1 John 1:10 reminds us of. We shouldn't pretend that we don't sin—that we're too good for sin now—because that's simply not true. We still sin. So what's different between us and those who haven't trusted in Jesus? Two things.

First, our sins are forgiven. The moment we trust in Jesus, all our sins—the ones we've already done and the ones we will still do—are forgiven. This is why God sees us as holy and perfect. Although our sin is forgiven, it's still dangerous. Sin hurts us and other people and it can hinder our relationship with God. When we sin, we don't feel as close to God, and that's never a good thing. Which takes us to the second big idea.

Because we've been made new in Jesus and we've been given the Holy Spirit, we have the power to fight against sin. We can look at sin differently and say no to it. We can see sin for what it really is, and we can grow to want no part of it. Sure, at times we might still be okay with sin in the moment and even enjoy it, but afterward, especially, we'll grieve our sins. Our sin will make us sad because we know we aren't living the way Jesus wants us to live and in the way that's best for him, us, and others. But through the Holy Spirit's guidance and power, we can turn from sin and live more and more like Jesus.

▶ What's a sin you've recently resisted?

DO CHRISTIANS SIN?

▶ How does it feel knowing all your sins are forgiven because of Jesus?

1 — 2 — 3 — 4 — 5 — 6 — 7 — 8 — 9 — 10

IT'S ALL RIGHT   IT'S AMAZING

▶ What questions do you have so far?

▶ What are you wondering about because of what you've heard?

PRAYER

God, thank you for forgiving all our sins, even the ones we do after trusting in Jesus. Amen.

FAMILY ACTIVITY: COMPETE

Do it. Make a favorite dessert, like ice cream sundaes or freshly baked cookies, and serve it to everyone. See who can hold out the longest before beginning to eat.

Discuss it. Talk about the strong pull we feel toward something we really want and how hard it can be to have willpower at times.

Connect it. Share that this is why we need God's help to resist sin. The Holy Spirit is always with us to make us stronger so we can say no to sin.

▼ JESUS CONNECTION ▼

Jesus was incredibly patient and gracious to people who recognized they'd sinned. He loved these people and wanted to help them turn to him for forgiveness and to the Holy Spirit to fight sin. We need to do the same with ourselves and others. We need to be kind, patient, and gracious, always remembering that fighting sin is a long, slow journey.

▶ How can you fight against sin this week?

45 HOW CAN CHRISTIANS RESIST SIN?

Christians can resist sin through the power of the Holy Spirit, by reading the Bible, and with the encouragement of other Christians.

PSALM 119:9-16 (OR 119:11)

If you were at the top of a high cliff with no guardrail, how close would you get to the edge? To be safest, you'd stay as far from the edge as possible, right? Why risk tripping or the ground giving way?

The same is true with sin. The best way to resist sin is by staying as far from it as possible. In fact, the Bible tells us to flee from sin—to run away from it! To be strong isn't getting as close to sin as possible without giving in; it's staying as far from sin as possible in the first place. Thankfully, God has given us three wonderful gifts to help us do just that.

First, God has given us the Holy Spirit. The Holy Spirit helps us see sin as the terrible thing it really is. Sin likes to play dress-up, disguising itself as something that will make us happy. But that's a lie. Sin will lead to trouble every single time. The Holy Spirit wants us to see this right away, before it's too late. He then does even more for us by giving us the power to say no to sin.

Second, God has given us the Bible. Filling our minds and hearts with what's good leaves no room for what's not good. This is what Psalm 119:11 tells us to do. When we're tempted to sin, one of the best ways to fight that desire is by reading the Bible.

Third, God gives us other Christians who can encourage and strengthen us. We are to love one another and help one another, knowing we are all in this together. At times we'll need help from others; at times we'll need to help others. Together, we're better.

▶ *What are you afraid of, like heights?*

▶ How comfortable are you asking others for help?

1 — 2 — 3 — 4 — 5 — 6 — 7 — 8 — 9 — 10
NO WAY, NO HOW   NO PROBLEM AT ALL

▶ What questions do you have so far?

▶ What are you wondering about because of what you've heard?

PRAYER

God, thank you for forgiving us and for giving us such amazing gifts to help us fight sin. Amen.

FAMILY ACTIVITY: CELEBRATE

Do it. Choose a Bible verse, such as Psalm 119:11, to memorize as a family. Work on it together, and once everyone has it memorized, celebrate with a fun night out or a special meal.

Discuss it. Talk about what you did to memorize the Bible verse and share tips and tricks with each other.

Connect it. Share how the Bible verse you memorized will be helpful as you each turn from sin and follow Jesus.

▼ JESUS CONNECTION ▼

Jesus showed us one of the greatest examples of how to fight sin when the devil tempted him in the wilderness. Each time, Jesus quoted the Bible to him. We can do the same, but that means we have to memorize parts of the Bible. Start with a few Bible verses, like Psalm 119:11, that can help you the most and work on memorizing them.

▶ **When will you work on memorizing a Bible verse this week and which one will it be?**

PART 5

SALVATION

MOST PEOPLE DON'T REALIZE IT, but the area of systematic theology they likely know the most about is soteriology, the study of salvation. That's because the most famous Bible verse—one even many non-Christians know—is John 3:16, and that's a verse about salvation.

It's not accidental that this section on salvation is located in the middle of The Family Catechism. It's the lynchpin to it all, just as Jesus and the salvation he provides is the center of the Bible and, indeed, the center of human history. Everything covered in the sections before this one builds up to it. And everything covered in the sections after this one flows from it. All The Family Catechism questions and answers matter, of course, but if there's one place you may want to slow down and make sure your child understands what's covered, it's this one.

This section begins by exploring the idea that sin has broken our relationship with God and there's nothing we can do about that. Notice there's nothing *we* can do. But that's not to say nothing can be done. God can certainly do something about our sin problem, and that's exactly what he did. Our loving, gracious, merciful, majestic, wonderful, holy, powerful God made a way—the only way—through Jesus. Salvation is thus a breathtaking mixture of initial despair and lasting hope.

Then, the bulk of this section walks through several key theological terms. While the words themselves are important, what they mean is far more important. The terms are presented in a logical order that aligns with the progression of salvation. It starts with God giving us grace and mercy, then it moves to us experiencing atonement, regeneration, justification, and adoption at the nanosecond of salvation. It then continues to our lifelong sanctification, and it culminates in our future glorification. In a sense, this series of questions provides a timeline of a person's salvation.

The section concludes with two critical questions. The first concerns what has been called "the great exchange," how Jesus has taken our sin from us and given us his righteousness in its place. While many of us understand the first part, that second part is often overlooked, but it's just as important and glorious.

Finally, the idea of assurance is explored from the perspective that no one who has truly trusted in Jesus and become a new creation can lose his or her salvation. Many believers live in fear that they can mess up somehow and lose their salvation, but that's not how God wants us to live. And that's not how we want our kids to live. Instead, God wants our children to live with peace, joy, and confidence. And so do we. That's the abundant living Jesus promised.

46 MUST WE DIE AND REMAIN SEPARATED FROM GOD BECAUSE OF SIN?

No. God has provided a way we can be forgiven of sin, be saved from death, and enjoy a relationship with him forever.

JOHN 3:16-18 (OR 3:16)

Thinking about sin isn't fun. It can be discouraging and even scary. Because of sin, every single person deserves to be separated from God forever. And there's nothing we can do about that. We're stuck; we can't get rid of our sin. In fact, instead of getting rid of our sin, we keep adding more to it. It's like we're in a sinking boat trying to empty it with a thimble while someone is filling the boat with a garden hose. We just can't win!

This is what we see in the first chapters of Genesis. Adam and Eve rebelled against God in Genesis 3. Cain killed Abel in Genesis 4. Death affected all people in Genesis 5. Then, in Genesis 6, the world got so bad that God sent a flood to wipe out people. Sin. Death. Destruction. That's rough! But God shows us something else in these chapters too: hope.

God gave Adam and Eve another son named Seth. There was one man—Enoch—who escaped death (Genesis 5:21-24). God didn't wipe everyone out by the flood; rather, he spared Noah and his family. This shows us that God takes sin seriously and judgment will come, but God also takes his love, mercy, and grace seriously. From the moment Adam and Eve sinned, God has been at work providing a way—the only way—to solve our sin problem. But not because of anything we do. It's because of what God has done. That solution is, of course, Jesus. That's what John 3:16 tells us—because God the Father loves us, he sent Jesus so that whoever believes in Jesus will be rescued from sin and death. All that we've broken because of sin Jesus has fixed!

▶ *Have you ever broken something, like a toy, that couldn't be fixed?*

▶ How does knowing there's a way to be forgiven of sin make you feel?

1 — 2 — 3 — 4 — 5 — 6 — 7 — 8 — 9 — 10
I GUESS IT'S OKAY   I KNOW IT'S AMAZING

▶ What questions do you have so far?

▶ What are you wondering about because of what you've heard?

PRAYER

God, thank you for making the way to forgive us of our sins when there seemed to be no way. Amen.

FAMILY ACTIVITY: PLAY

Do it. Play a game like Phase 10, Chutes and Ladders, or Candy Land in which a player can fall well behind the others.

Discuss it. Talk about how it feels to be stuck and without hope in a game.

Connect it. Declare everyone a winner and share that this is what God has done for all who have trusted in Jesus.

▼ JESUS CONNECTION ▼

Jesus didn't need to be forgiven of sin, because he never sinned. But Jesus didn't remain in heaven, shaking his head in disgust because of our sins. Instead, he stepped forward to help us. He came to earth and gave up his life for us. That's love! We can treat others the same way. We can't forgive anyone's sins, but we can lovingly point them to the one who can.

▶ Who can you tell about Jesus' love and forgiveness this week?

47

HOW CAN WE BE FORGIVEN OF SIN AND HAVE A RELATIONSHIP WITH GOD FOREVER?

We can be forgiven of sin and have a relationship with God forever only through faith in Jesus.

ROMANS 10:13-17 (OR 10:13)

As you read the Bible, you might notice different ways people tried to deal with their sin problem to be right with God. Some people thought if they worshiped God, he would be happy with them even if they worshiped other gods too. Other people believed God was okay with them simply because they were born into the right family or people group. Still others counted on doing enough good things to be right with God.

None of these worked, though. We can't worship our way to God. That doesn't take care of our sin problem. It doesn't matter what people group we are part of—all people are sinful and need salvation. And no amount of good can undo the wrong we do.

Thankfully, God provided a way—*the* way—to be right with him. Romans 10:13 tells us what that one and only way is: faith in Jesus. In Eden, God said a descendant of Adam and Eve's would come and crush the serpent and win the victory (Genesis 3:15). Jesus is that descendant. He is the Rescuer who came to earth and crushed sin and death under his foot. Anyone who puts their faith in Jesus is forgiven. But how do we do this?

First, we admit that we sin and that because of our sin we deserve to be separated from God. Then, we recognize that Jesus is the Son of God, the sinless Rescuer sent by the Father. He lived a perfect life, died in our place, and rose from the grave. Finally, we trust that Jesus paid the penalty for our sins and we accept the gift of forgiveness. That's how we are saved; that's the only way we can be saved. God is so good for making a way!

▶ *What are some ways people today try to be right with God?*

HOW CAN WE BE FORGIVEN AND A FRIEND OF GOD?

▶ How much faith have you placed in Jesus to forgive your sins?

1 — 2 — 3 — 4 — 5 — 6 — 7 — 8 — 9 — 10
NONE AT ALL · · · · · · · · · ALL OF IT

▶ What questions do you have so far?

▶ What are you wondering about because of what you've heard?

PRAYER

God, thank you for providing Jesus to forgive our sins so we can be your friends. Amen.

FAMILY ACTIVITY: GATHER

Do it. Invite several Christian friends over for dinner or dessert.

Discuss it. Ask your guests to share their stories of how they first trusted in Jesus and how they continue to walk in faith. Ask what lessons or tips they can offer.

Connect it. Share how we each might have different stories of how we trusted in Jesus, but Jesus is at the center of them all.

▼ JESUS CONNECTION ▼

Having faith can be difficult. We tend to think it was easy for Jesus to trust in the Father, but it was hard for him at times too—like when he was praying in the garden just before his arrest. But through it all, Jesus held onto complete trust in the Father and his ways. When we take steps of faith—big or small—we're walking like Jesus!

▶ *What step of faith can you take this week?*

48 WHAT DOES IT MEAN TO BE RIGHTEOUS?

To be righteous means to obey God fully and to please him in how we live.

MATTHEW 5:17-20 (OR 5:20)

The thing about true-false questions is they're either right or wrong. There's no in between. A right answer earns full credit; a wrong answer earns no credit. It's that simple. Following God is sort of like that. We're either right with God or we're not. We either obey God or we don't. When we obey God and are right with him, that's called being righteous.

We are to be righteous in all we do. In every decision we make, every word we say, and everything we even think, we're to obey God and please him. So, for example, God has told us not to steal (Exodus 20:15). When you don't steal a friend's piece of gum, you've obeyed this command. You've pleased God and acted righteously. Or, God has said we're not to lie (Exodus 20:16). When you're asked who ate the last cookie and you tell the truth that you did, you're obeying God. You're pleasing him.

If life were like one big true-false test, it would mean we'd have hundreds—even thousands—of questions to answer every day. To be righteous would be to act righteously in each one. Not most of them. All of them. It would be getting each day's true-false test perfectly right. Day after day, week after week, and year after year.

This is what Jesus meant when he said his followers had to be more righteous than the Pharisees. The Pharisees were thought to be elite followers of God. They did get things right, but they didn't get everything right, and that simply wasn't enough. God expects perfection from us. We can't be righteous on our own, but thankfully God made a way for us to be righteous. When we trust in Jesus, we become fully righteous!

▶ **What sort of test do you like the least? The most?**

WHAT DOES IT MEAN TO BE RIGHTEOUS?

▶ How righteous were you today?

1 — 2 — 3 — 4 — 5 — 6 — 7 — 8 — 9 — 10
I COMPLETELY FAILED   I PASSED WITH FLYING COLORS

▶ What questions do you have so far?

▶ What are you wondering about because of what you've heard?

PRAYER

God, thank you for creating us to live for you in all our ways. Amen.

FAMILY ACTIVITY: EXPLORE

Do it. Go for a drive and use a mapping app.

Discuss it. Talk about how mapping apps are usually right, but at times they can give bad directions.

Connect it. Share that God isn't like a mapping app. He always gives the right directions so we can obey him with full confidence.

▼ JESUS CONNECTION ▼

While Jesus was on earth, he fully obeyed the Father in all he did. The Gospels give us details of only a few years of his life (and even those don't tell us all he did), but we know in every way—big and small—Jesus obeyed. That's the example we're to follow. Our goal each day, and each minute of the day, is to obey God and live the way he made us to live.

▶ What can you do in the next hour to be righteous?

49 CAN WE BE SAVED BY OUR OWN RIGHTEOUSNESS?

No. No one is righteous enough on his or her own to be saved.

ROMANS 3:10-18 (OR 3:10)

Everyone can do good. Even the worst, most evil person you can think of can perform an act of kindness. No one does bad things one hundred percent of the time. Some get closer to that than others, but everyone does at least some good here and there. The problem is that none of us can do good all the time. We can be righteous at times, but we can't be righteous all the time. That's what Romans 3:10 tells us. And that's the problem: even the best of us still sin. And no amount of good can undo that sin.

It's like putting a teeny-tiny drop of poison in a cup of drinking water. You can add more water, sugar, or whatever else you want to it, but that poison will still be there. You simply can't add enough good things to the water to remove that one very, very bad thing. Or it's like using a permanent marker on a dry erase board. You can't undo it. You can color around it and over it, but that permanent marker will still be there.

That's what even the smallest amount of sin does to us. Unfortunately, God doesn't grade us on a curve. We don't pass if we make just a few mistakes. As long as we have even a single sin—a single teeny-tiny drop of poison or a permanent mark—we aren't holy. And because we aren't holy, we deserve God's judgment. No amount of good we can do can ever undo our sin. But the great news is that God did something to take care of it for us. He gave us Jesus!

▶ *Who is the kindest, best person you can think of?*

CAN WE BE SAVED BY OUR OWN RIGHTEOUSNESS?

▶ **How do you think you rank in terms of doing good things?**

1 — 2 — 3 — 4 — 5 — 6 — 7 — 8 — 9 — 10

AMONG THE WORST   AMONG THE BEST

▶ **What questions do you have so far?**

▶ **What are you wondering about because of what you've heard?**

PRAYER

God, thank you for providing Jesus, the righteous one, as the only way we can be saved. Amen.

FAMILY ACTIVITY: PLAY

Do it. Play Simon Says, being sure to make the game increasingly difficult.

Discuss it. Talk about the challenges of playing the game. Even when we're paying close attention and trying really hard, we can still mess up.

Connect it. Share how it's hard to do what's right, even when we really want to, which is why God has given us the Holy Spirit to help us.

▼ JESUS CONNECTION ▼

Only one person ever was completely righteous: Jesus. Jesus did nothing at all wrong. Then, because he loves us so much, he died to pay a punishment he didn't deserve to give us salvation we don't deserve. We can't die for anyone else's sins, but we can pray for them and point them to how Jesus can save them.

▶ **Who do you know that needs to trust in Jesus and that you can pray for this week?**

50 WHO, THEN, WILL BE SAVED?

Everyone who repents of their sins and trusts in Jesus will be saved.

ACTS 2:23-41 (OR 2:38)

We're all sinners. None of us are righteous like we need to be. And that's a problem. A big one! If this sin problem were up to us to solve, we'd be stuck without a solution. We'd be forever scrubbing and scrubbing at a permanent marker on a dry erase board without making any difference at all. We simply can't undo our sin. We can't hide it. We can't excuse it. People in the Bible tried to undo, hide, and excuse their sins, but it never worked.

Thankfully, it's not up to us. What we can't do God has done. God fixed what we broke and he made a way—*the* way—for our sins to be dealt with and for us to be saved from judgment.

This is what Peter explained to the crowd gathered at Pentecost in Acts 2. After talking about how people are sinful and Jesus is the promised Messiah—the Rescuer—the people responded by asking him a wonderful question: "What must we do?" The crowd understood they had a problem, and they also seemed to understand they didn't have the answer to their problem. They needed help from someone else.

And that's the key to salvation. We must recognize we have a sin problem we can't fix. We then go to the only one who can fix it: Jesus. He did all the work to fix things on our behalf. All we must do is repent of our sins—to turn away from sin and toward Jesus—and trust in him. And then our sin—that dark permanent marker—is taken completely away, gone forevermore. God is so good to us, isn't he?

▶ *What are some things we can't do without someone's help?*

WHO, THEN, WILL BE SAVED?

▶ **How do you feel about Jesus fixing your sin problem?**

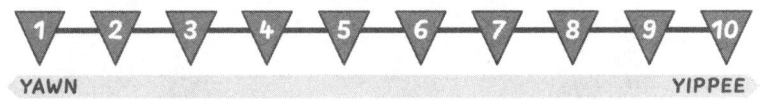

1 — 2 — 3 — 4 — 5 — 6 — 7 — 8 — 9 — 10
YAWN   YIPPEE

▶ **What questions do you have so far?**

▶ **What are you wondering about because of what you've heard?**

PRAYER

God, thank you for Jesus providing the forgiveness of sins we don't deserve. Amen.

FAMILY ACTIVITY: PLAY

Do it. Try to solve a few complicated wooden puzzles, do an escape room together, or share some difficult riddles.

Discuss it. Talk about the challenges you faced and how frustrating it can be to have a problem that can't be solved.

Connect it. Share how amazing it is that God solved our greatest problem of sin on our behalf. Through trusting in Jesus, we escape judgment!

▼ JESUS CONNECTION ▼

When we think about how we can't do anything to fix our sin problem but Jesus has done everything, it reminds us of how generous he is. He gave up his life for us—there's no greater gift than that. As we follow in Jesus' ways, we can make it our goal to be as generous as possible, showing others a glimpse of Jesus' amazing generosity.

▶ **Who can you give a small gift to this week to show a picture of what Jesus has done?**

51 WHAT DOES IT MEAN TO REPENT?

To repent means to be grieved by sin and to turn away from it.

2 CHRONICLES 7:11-14 (OR 7:14)

Imagine you're riding your bike to a friend's house and you realize you're going the wrong way. In fact, you're going the exact opposite direction from where you need to go! What would you do? Most likely, you would stop, turn around, and head the correct direction instead.

That's a picture of what it means to repent. Only we aren't talking about riding our bikes any longer; we're talking about living the right way. From the day we're born, we're heading in the wrong direction. Instead of heading toward God, we're heading away from him. That's because of our sin. We just keep moving farther away from God, continuing to go our own way.

But then, when the Holy Spirit helps us realize the seriousness of our sin, we should first grieve that sin. To grieve means to feel sorry that we've disobeyed God. But we don't stop there. We then choose something different. We choose to turn away from our sin. Just like we'd stop and turn around on our bikes, we stop and turn from our sin and turn toward Jesus instead. That's repentance. We choose to get as far from sin as we can because we know it hurts us and, more importantly, it dishonors God.

But we don't turn in just any direction. We turn from going in the wrong direction—toward sin—to go in the right direction—toward God. And the wonderful thing is that God is always ready and willing to accept us! That's what he told the Israelites in 2 Chronicles 7; it's never too late to turn from sin and turn back to him. That's true of us too. We can always repent, choosing to follow Jesus instead of chasing after our own sin. And that's always a great choice!

▶ *If you could design the perfect bike, what fun things would you add to it?*

WHAT DOES IT MEAN TO REPENT?

▶ *How good are you at turning away from sin?*

1 — 2 — 3 — 4 — 5 — 6 — 7 — 8 — 9 — 10

NOT SO GOOD — VERY GOOD

▶ *What questions do you have so far?*

▶ *What are you wondering about because of what you've heard?*

PRAYER

God, thank you that Jesus came so we can turn toward him rather than continuing in our sins. Amen.

FAMILY ACTIVITY: PLAY

Do it. Play UNO.

Discuss it. Each time someone plays a Reverse card, pause and share one sin we can repent of and one reason why it's better to turn to Jesus.

Connect it. Share how we have opportunities to repent every day and that God is always waiting with open arms for us to turn to him.

▼ JESUS CONNECTION ▼

Jesus didn't have to repent of sin because he never sinned. However, that doesn't mean he didn't recognize the seriousness of sin and the hurt it causes. He saw this hurt in others, and he responded in love, trying to help others recognize their sins and repent. We need to repent of our own sin, but we can live like Jesus by also helping others do the same.

▶ *What is something you can do to help you repent the next time you sin?*

52 WHAT IS GRACE?

Grace is God lovingly giving us good things we don't deserve.

EPHESIANS 2:4-10 (OR 2:8-9)

To understand grace, we first need to understand what a gift is. A gift is something we're given that we didn't earn or that we didn't do anything to deserve. When we think of gifts, we often think of Christmas or birthday presents. But the problem is, we sort of think we deserve those gifts. Imagine how you'd feel if you didn't get any presents on your birthday or Christmas. You'd feel wronged, wouldn't you? You'd feel like everyone failed to do what they were supposed to do—give you a gift. In fact, you might feel like you earned some Christmas gifts by being good during the year. So let's not think of those gifts.

Instead, have you ever been given a "just because" gift? Someone gave you an amazing gift simply because that person loves you? That's what God's grace is like. Because of his great love for us, God gives us many good things without us doing anything to earn or deserve them. God gives us these gifts—he gives us grace—just because he loves us and it pleases him to give them to us.

In a sense, every good thing we have—our families, our possessions, our lives even—are given to us by God's grace. Those are all fantastic, for sure. But by far, the greatest gift of grace God has given us is Jesus and the forgiveness he provides. This is what Paul talks about in Ephesians 2. We deserve terrible things because of our sin, but God gives us wonderful things, namely Jesus, because of his loving grace. We didn't earn or deserve Jesus; we earned and deserve judgment. But God gave us Jesus all the same. That's love. That's grace. That's wonderful, loving, amazing grace!

▶ **What's the best gift you've ever been given?**

WHAT IS GRACE?

▶ How do you feel about the love and forgiveness God has given you?

| 1 | 2 | 3 | 4 | 5 | 6 | 7 | 8 | 9 | 10 |

I'VE EARNED IT   IT'S A GIFT

▶ What questions do you have so far?

▶ What are you wondering about because of what you've heard?

PRAYER

God, thank you for your good, loving grace that you pour out on us and that will never ever run out. Amen.

FAMILY ACTIVITY: CELEBRATE

Do it. Set up a gift exchange for your family, or choose someone outside your family to give a generous gift to just because you care about them.

Discuss it. Talk about the joy of giving and receiving gifts.

Connect it. Share how we've been given the greatest gift ever in Jesus.

▼ JESUS CONNECTION ▼

Grace and generosity go hand in hand. Jesus provides the best example of both. He was full of love and grace for people and he was also amazingly generous—even giving his very life for others. As we try to live like Jesus, we want to be as gracious and giving to others as we can be. Even if we don't have much, we can still be generous with whatever we have.

▶ How can you be gracious this week and give someone something they didn't earn?

53

WHAT IS MERCY?

Mercy is God lovingly not giving us the punishment we deserve.

1 SAMUEL 24:2-11 (OR 24:7)

You might remember how David rescued King Saul and Israel by defeating a giant named Goliath (1 Samuel 17). Saul was thankful at first, but he soon became jealous of David's fame. He even tried to kill David, so David along with some loyal friends went into hiding.

When Saul and his army chased after David, they stopped near a cave David and his friends were in. Then Saul went into that cave by himself! He was alone and defenseless. David had the perfect opportunity to kill him. If he did, David and his friends would be safe and they could return to their families and go back to normal life.

We can't forget that Saul was in the wrong; David was innocent. We also can't forget that God had promised that David would become king. Was this moment arranged by God for that to happen? No, it wasn't! David refused to kill Saul. He simply couldn't find it within himself to harm God's king, even if that king wanted to harm him and even if God had chosen David to replace that king. God would make that happen, not David. Later, David even had a second chance to harm Saul, but he didn't then either (1 Samuel 26).

David sparing Saul's life is a wonderful picture of mercy—not giving someone a bad thing they deserve. Grace and mercy are opposites that work together. We deserve God's punishment (a bad thing) for our sins, but God doesn't punish us (mercy). At the same time, God gives us forgiveness (a good thing) that we don't deserve (grace). But God's mercy and grace go beyond that. Because God loves us so much, he continues to withhold all sorts of bad things from us while showering many good things on us.

▶ If you had to face a giant or an angry king, which would you choose?

WHAT IS MERCY?

▶ How aware of God's mercy and grace are you each day?

1 — 2 — 3 — 4 — 5 — 6 — 7 — 8 — 9 — 10

NEVER — ALWAYS

▶ What questions do you have so far?

▶ What are you wondering about because of what you've heard?

PRAYER

God, thank you for loving us and giving us mercy instead of punishment for sin. Amen.

FAMILY ACTIVITY: GATHER

Do it. Think of a least favorite meal and tell your family it will be served for dinner. At the last minute, share that no one has to eat that meal, and serve a cake or favorite dessert for dinner instead.

Discuss it. Talk about what it felt like to be spared from having to eat the original meal, and what it was like to have dessert for dinner instead.

Connect it. Share how God is so good to give us both mercy and grace.

▼ JESUS CONNECTION ▼

At the root of mercy is love. It's God's love for us that keeps him from punishing us, and it's his love that led to Jesus being punished in our place. When we think about love and mercy, it's easy to see how Jesus modeled both. On the cross, he could have called angels to come punish those who lied about him, beat him, and crucified him. But he didn't. He let love and mercy carry the day. And so can we.

▶ How can you show someone mercy this week?

54 WHAT IS ATONEMENT?

Atonement is how Jesus made us right with God by paying our sin penalty.

LEVITICUS 16:15-22 (OR 16:16)

Atonement is a big word we don't use very often. We find a hint to what it means right in the word, though: "at-one-ment." To be "at one" with someone is to be at peace with them. So atonement means we're brought into peace with God. But to be brought into peace with God must mean we didn't start that way.

We live in a broken world and we have a broken relationship with God, at least to start with. But that's our fault. We wronged God; he didn't wrong us. That's why we deserve God's judgment for our sins. And that's why we should be the ones to fix our broken relationship. We made the mess; we should clean it up. But we can't. There's nothing we can do to fix what we broke.

So what did God do? Because he loves us, he fixed things for us. Although he was the one wronged, he did what it took to make things right. This is why Jesus came to earth to live the perfect life we failed to live and to pay the penalty for sin we couldn't pay. This is how Jesus has made atonement for us.

This is what the Day of Atonement, explained in Leviticus 16, is all about. It was a picture of what Jesus would do. The high priest symbolically placed the sins of the people on two goats. The first goat was killed and its blood sprinkled inside the tabernacle. The second goat was run off into the wilderness. Those two goats picture Jesus. He gave up his life for us to cover our sins, and then all our sins were taken away from us forevermore. And because of that, we are now at one with God again. We have atonement!

▶ *What is the biggest word you know?*

WHAT IS ATONEMENT? 123

▶ *How does Jesus making atonement for you make you feel?*

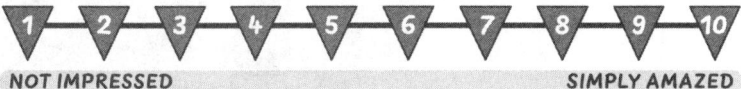

1 — 2 — 3 — 4 — 5 — 6 — 7 — 8 — 9 — 10

NOT IMPRESSED   SIMPLY AMAZED

▶ *What questions do you have so far?*

▶ *What are you wondering about because of what you've heard?*

PRAYER

God, thank you for providing Jesus to forgive our sins and make atonement for us. Amen.

FAMILY ACTIVITY: CREATE

Do it. Build a model or assemble a puzzle.

Discuss it. As you work, talk about how what you are working on began in many different pieces, but you're making it one.

Connect it. Share how what you're doing is a picture of what Jesus has done for us, only what he did happened instantly when we trusted in him.

▼ JESUS CONNECTION ▼

Jesus gave up his life so we could be brought back together with God. To live like Jesus means we'll do our best to fix our relationships with others when needed. It also means we'll help others fix their relationships with each other, but most importantly, it means we'll help others turn to Jesus' atonement to have their relationship with God fixed too.

▶ *What can you do this week to help fix or strengthen a relationship you have with someone or one between others you know?*

55

WHAT IS REGENERATION?

Regeneration is the Holy Spirit giving us a new heart that loves God and wants to obey him.

EZEKIEL 36:24-30 (OR 36:26)

Sin has made our hearts work not like they should. That doesn't mean your heart doesn't pump blood throughout your body the right way. We're not talking about the heart beating inside your chest. We're talking about the heart that symbolizes your innermost desires. We usually want most whatever pleases us most. We want to make ourselves happy above anything else, including making God happy.

But that's not what God wants from us. Oh, he wants us to be happy, for sure. But he wants us to be happy in the right way—by living in a way that pleases him, which is also good for us. Our hearts, though, struggle to do that.

That's why we need a new heart, one that isn't broken by sin. We need a new heart that wants what God wants. We need a new heart that puts God first. We need a new heart that loves God the most instead of loving anything else the most.

Thankfully, that's exactly what we get when we trust in Jesus. As the prophet Ezekiel tells us, God removes our heart of stone—a hard heart that is often against God—and replaces it with a soft heart—one that is tender to responding to God. Because God gives us this wonderful new heart, we're able to obey God like he deserves. We can finally live the way we were made to live. That's why this is called *regeneration*, a big word that means "new life." It's also why trusting in Jesus is called being "born again." Because of Jesus, we become new people who love and obey God!

▶ Which do you like better: cookies that are chewy and soft or ones that are crispy and hard?

WHAT IS REGENERATION?

▶ **What is your heart like toward God?**

1 — 2 — 3 — 4 — 5 — 6 — 7 — 8 — 9 — 10

STONE · · · · · · · · · SOFT

▶ **What questions do you have so far?**

▶ **What are you wondering about because of what you've heard?**

PRAYER

God, thank you for taking our hard hearts away and replacing them with soft hearts that love you and want to obey you. Amen.

FAMILY ACTIVITY: CELEBRATE

Do it. Even if it isn't anyone's birthday or adoption day, have a birthday or adoption celebration.

Discuss it. Share the story of your child's birth, adoption, or the way he or she came to be part of your family. Talk about how your lives have changed because of that wonderful addition.

Connect it. Share how this is a picture of what it's like to have new life through Jesus.

▼ JESUS CONNECTION ▼

Jesus shows us what it looks like to love God. Jesus didn't focus on himself while he was on earth; rather, he focused on pleasing the Father. And Jesus' love for the Father led him to love people too. As we seek to live like Jesus, the most important thing we can do is love God. And when we do that, like Jesus, we'll love others.

▶ *How can you show a parent, sibling, friend, or neighbor that you love them this week?*

56 WHAT IS JUSTIFICATION?

Justification is God declaring that we are forgiven of our sins and that we are righteous.

ROMANS 5:1-2 (OR 5:1)

Have you ever seen a show or movie in which a person who was charged with a crime was in court to hear a judge's verdict? You probably saw the accused person standing up and then the judge or another court official reading the charges against him. At this point, things can go in one of two directions. The judge can say "guilty," which means the judge believes the person did the crime. The person on trial would then be punished appropriately. Or the judge can say "not guilty." That means the judge wasn't convinced that the person did the crime. And if that happens, the person is free to go. He came into the courtroom in handcuffs and under guard, but he's then completely free to walk out on his own. All because the judge said so.

That's what happens when we trust in Jesus. The instant we place our faith in Jesus, God declares us "not guilty." Seconds before, we were trapped by sin and we deserved to be punished for it. But in the blink of an eye, God says that's no longer true about us. Instead, he says we're forgiven and that we're righteous.

That's what Romans 5:1 is about. In Christ, God declares us righteous, and just like that, we have peace with God! It's just like we've never sinned. And that's how you can remember what justified means: God makes it "just as if I'd" never sinned. In the moment our amazing God did this, we were set free. We were finally free from sin and free to live the way God made us to live. Isn't it wonderful to have a God who loves us that much?

▶ Would you rather be a judge or a lawyer? Why?

WHAT IS JUSTIFICATION?

▶ *How much do you need God's forgiveness?*

1 — 2 — 3 — 4 — 5 — 6 — 7 — 8 — 9 — 10

JUST A LITTLE   QUITE A LOT

▶ *What questions do you have so far?*

▶ *What are you wondering about because of what you've heard?*

PRAYER

God, thank you for saying we are no longer guilty of sin the moment we trusted in Jesus. Amen.

FAMILY ACTIVITY: EXPERIMENT

Do it. Judge different kinds of snacks, desserts, or something else your family enjoys. If possible, sample each one while you judge the different items and determine which is the best.

Discuss it. Talk about what standards you used to judge the items. Were they the same for everyone?

Connect it. Share how God doesn't judge us the way you judged the items—he forgives us based only on what Jesus has done!

▼ JESUS CONNECTION ▼

While Jesus was on earth, one thing he did was tell people about how they could be forgiven by God. He explained that when a person trusts in him, they are forgiven and God declares them not guilty. We can't say someone is forgiven—only God can do that—but we can live like Jesus and tell as many people as we can about how they can find forgiveness through Jesus.

▶ *Who will you tell about God's amazing forgiveness through Jesus this week?*

57 WHAT IS ADOPTION?

Adoption is God bringing us into his forever family as his children.

ROMANS 8:14-17 (OR 8:15)

To be adopted is to be brought into a family that wasn't yours to begin with. But adoption doesn't mean you're brought partly into a new family. It doesn't even mean you're brought mostly into a family. When you're adopted, you're brought *entirely* into a family. You aren't *like* a son or daughter; you *become* a son or daughter. Fully. Completely. Without exception and with no fine print. When you're adopted it's just as if you were born into that family to begin with and it has been your family all along. Adoption is all about wonderful love and acceptance!

This is what Romans 8 says God does for us when we trust in Jesus. The split second we trust in Jesus as our Rescuer, our marvelous God adopts us into his family as his beloved children. And in that moment, we don't become like his children. We don't become somewhat or mostly his children. We become *fully* his children.

This means we get to call the Creator of the universe our loving Father, just like Jesus did! This means we are loved and accepted entirely by our gracious God and his love and acceptance for us will never end. It means we can stand firm in the promises our faithful God has made to us—promises like how he has forgiven us and how we'll spend forever with him. Never think our God is a cold, distant boss who we must obey or else we'll get into trouble. Instead, remember that God is our loving, warm, generous Father who delights in us as we delight in him.

▶ *If you could adopt anyone to become part of your family, who would that be?*

- How safe do you feel knowing you will always be part of God's family?

  1 — 2 — 3 — 4 — 5 — 6 — 7 — 8 — 9 — 10
  NOT AT ALL   COMPLETELY

- What questions do you have so far?

- What are you wondering about because of what you've heard?

PRAYER

God, thank you for adopting us into your forever family and for being our loving Father. Amen.

FAMILY ACTIVITY: SERVE

Do it. Volunteer at a pet adoption organization, or if that isn't possible, visit a pet store.

Discuss it. Talk about how the pets will be so happy when they're adopted by a loving family, and so will the family.

Connect it. Show how that happiness doesn't come close to the joy we have knowing that God has adopted us.

▼ JESUS CONNECTION ▼

The amazing thing about God's family is that there's always room for more! While Jesus was on earth, he spent his time trying to grow God's family. He wanted everyone to trust in him and be adopted by God. To live like Jesus means we'll do the same; we'll want as many people as possible to become part of God's family as our brothers and sisters.

- Who can you pray for this week that they might become part of God's family?

58 WHAT IS SANCTIFICATION?

Sanctification is gradually growing to live more like Jesus.

GENESIS 32:24-31 (OR 32:28)

Jacob wasn't the nicest person. When his twin brother Esau was hungry, instead of giving him something to eat, Jacob made Esau trade the family birthright for some stew. Later, he tricked their father and stole Esau's family blessing. This made Esau so angry that Jacob had to run away, breaking their family apart. Why would God choose to use a person like Jacob? Because Jacob didn't stay like that. God was working in him to change him and make him the person he was made to be.

That's what the wrestling match in Genesis 32 was all about. God wanted to show that Jacob was always wrestling and fighting to get his way. But Jacob didn't need to do that. Instead, he needed to learn to be humble and trust in God. Jacob didn't learn this lesson perfectly, but from this time on, he gradually changed for the better.

When we trust in Jesus, we become new people. We look the same and feel the same, and we might even act the same at first, but the truth is we aren't the same anymore. The Holy Spirit regenerates us—he gives us a new heart that wants to love and obey God. But we don't love and obey God perfectly right away. It's not like a light switch we flick on. Instead, it's a long, slow process of growing to be more like Jesus. This process of growth is called *sanctification*. We might not be able to tell much difference day by day, but, like Jacob, we can look back at who we were last week, last month, or last year and see how God is lovingly and patiently shaping us to be more like Jesus.

▶ What would you be willing to trade for your all-time favorite food?

WHAT IS SANCTIFICATION?

▶ How much have you grown to be like Jesus?

1 — 2 — 3 — 4 — 5 — 6 — 7 — 8 — 9 — 10

I'M JUST STARTING — I'VE ARRIVED

▶ What questions do you have so far?

▶ What are you wondering about because of what you've heard?

PRAYER

God, thank you for loving us enough to change us and for being so patient with us as we grow. Amen.

FAMILY ACTIVITY: EXPLORE

Do it. Go to a barbecue restaurant or look at smokers in a store.

Discuss it. Talk about how smokers cook meat at a low temperature over many hours, and that process cannot be rushed. "Low and slow" is the key.

Connect it. Share how God most often grows us "low and slow" to be more like Jesus through sanctification.

▼ JESUS CONNECTION ▼

During his time on earth, Jesus said "follow me" quite often. He always looked for people who were willing to believe in him and to live like him. We can't miss that last part. Our amazing journey as Christians doesn't end when we trust in Jesus, it only begins! From that day on, God patiently helps us grow to follow Jesus by living more and more like him.

▶ What's one area of your life that you can ask God to help you grow to be more like Jesus?

59 WHAT IS GLORIFICATION?

Glorification is when God will make everything perfect in the restored creation.

PHILIPPIANS 3:17-21 (OR 3:20-21)

Many wonderful things happen the instant we're saved. God justifies us, declaring that we're fully forgiven and righteous, and he adopts us into his forever family as his sons and daughters. We become a new creation, made new in the image of Jesus. And the Holy Spirit begins helping us live out our new identity in Jesus. But we still live in a broken world that is full of pain and hurt, and we'll continue to give in to sin, even if we don't do that as much as time goes on. Sometimes, following Jesus can feel frustrating or even disappointing. It's at times like these, especially, when it's helpful to remember the hope of glorification we have.

Our lives are much, much better than they were before we trusted in Jesus, but they're still not as good as they could be. The good news is, though, that our lives aren't as good as they will be. This is what Paul wanted the Philippian Christians to understand. Life in Philippi was difficult for these believers, just like our lives at times can be difficult for us. But Paul wanted the Philippians and us to know that something better is coming.

One day, Jesus will return and he will fix everything sin has broken. One day, Jesus will end sin, pain, suffering, and death for good. Jesus will make a new heaven and earth, and all the bad things that are here now because of sin will be gone forever. There will be no sickness or disease. No poverty or hunger. No natural disasters. No disobeying God or hurting one another. Everything will be perfect—the way God originally made it to be and how he has always meant it to be. This is all true!

▶ *What do you think God's perfect new world will be like?*

WHAT IS GLORIFICATION?

▶ How do you feel about Jesus returning and making a new heaven and earth?

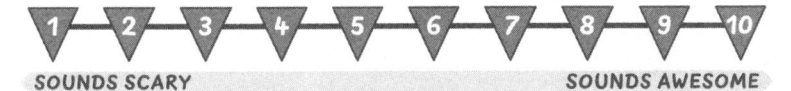

1 — 2 — 3 — 4 — 5 — 6 — 7 — 8 — 9 — 10
SOUNDS SCARY   SOUNDS AWESOME

▶ What questions do you have so far?

▶ What are you wondering about because of what you've heard?

PRAYER

God, thank you for promising that a day is coming when you will fix everything that has been broken by sin. Amen.

FAMILY ACTIVITY: CREATE

Do it. Find an old, broken-down item to restore.

Discuss it. Talk about what the item was probably like when it was brand-new and how close you think you'll come to restoring it.

Connect it. Share how one day Jesus will return and restore everything to be just as it was meant to be.

▼ JESUS CONNECTION ▼

When Jesus came to earth, he showed a glimpse of what the world is supposed to be like. He loved, fed, and healed people and he celebrated God in everything he did. We can't do all that Jesus did, but like him, we can do our best to show others what the world is supposed to be like. When we love like Jesus and care for others, we show a picture of the world that is coming one day!

▶ How can you love and care for someone this week?

60

WHAT DOES JESUS TAKE FROM US AND GIVE TO US WHEN WE ARE SAVED?

When we are saved, Jesus takes our sin from us and gives us his righteousness.

2 CORINTHIANS 5:18-21 (OR 5:21)

There have been some bad trades in sports. Teams have traded superstars for players who would play poorly or never even play for their new teams. Of course, both teams thought they were getting a good return in the trade, but it simply didn't work out that way. These trades are known as "one-sided" trades because one team got all the good value from the trade while the other team got almost nothing. Of all the one-sided trades, one stands out the most—but it wasn't a sports trade. The most one-sided trade ever was the one Jesus made with us when we trusted in him and were saved. Paul tells us about this trade in 2 Corinthians 5.

In this trade, we gave Jesus all our sins—every sin we did to that point, every sin we've done since, and every sin we will do in the future. If that wasn't one-sided enough, Jesus gave us something amazing in return: his perfect righteousness. Jesus gave us the credit for his life of perfect obedience. Now that's a one-sided trade!

Why would Jesus make this trade? Because he loves us and wants to please the Father! This trade is necessary for the gospel to work. Our sins must be dealt with. So Jesus took those sins from us and paid their penalty on the cross. But at the same time, in Eden, God made it clear that he doesn't just require us not to sin; he also requires us to obey him. Being forgiven of our sin takes care of the first half but not the second half. But because we have been credited with Jesus' perfect righteousness, we can stand before God completely obedient too. If you ever doubt God's love for you, just remember this trade!

▶ *What is a trade you wish you could make?*

WHAT DOES JESUS TAKE FROM US AND GIVE TO US?

▶ Which means more to you: Jesus taking away your sins or him giving his righteousness to you?

1 — 2 — 3 — 4 — 5 — 6 — 7 — 8 — 9 — 10

TAKING MY SINS   GIVING HIS RIGHTEOUSNESS

▶ What questions do you have so far?

▶ What are you wondering about because of what you've heard?

PRAYER

God, thank you for Jesus coming to make such an amazing trade with us. Amen.

FAMILY ACTIVITY: VISIT

Do it. Visit a swap meet, flea market, sporting card show, or some event where trading occurs. Try to get a good deal on an item, and then try to make the worst possible deal for yourself.

Discuss it. Talk about how hard it is to make a selfless trade; we usually want the best for ourselves.

Connect it. Share how making a selfless trade is a picture of what Jesus did for us.

▼ JESUS CONNECTION ▼

In a way, our trade with Jesus wasn't actually one-sided. We got a lot from Jesus, but he got a lot too—the Father was pleased with him! Jesus' humility, sacrifice, and love bring great glory to the Father, especially when someone trusts in him for salvation. As we look to live like Jesus, we can pursue similar humility, sacrifice, and love—always looking for how we can put someone else's good before our own.

▶ Who can you humbly serve this week even if it costs you something?

61

CAN THOSE WHO HAVE TRUSTED IN JESUS LOSE THEIR SALVATION AND BREAK THEIR RELATIONSHIP WITH GOD?

No. All who have trusted in Jesus can do nothing to lose their salvation and break their relationship with God.

JOHN 10:27-30 (OR 10:28)

Grammar is the rules of how a language works. These rules can be quite technical and they can get confusing. While some people love grammar, many people aren't really fans of it. But grammar is important. It allows us to communicate well with others, and it also helps us understand the Bible. It's always important to read the Bible carefully, but sometimes it's even more important. If we don't, we can miss what a verse means. This is especially true of John 10:28.

In John 10:28, Jesus said something important about those who trust in him: "I give them eternal life, and they will never perish." Notice Jesus didn't say that he gives those who trust in him the "opportunity to have" eternal life so they "might not" perish. Neither did he say that he gives eternal life and they will never perish "if they do certain things" or "if they don't do other things." No, what Jesus said is clear: he gives eternal life. And eternal, by definition, is forever.

The second you trusted in Jesus, you received eternal, everlasting, forever, always-and-without-end life! It's locked in. If it could be taken away or lost, it wouldn't be eternal life, would it? But it *is* eternal life, which is why Jesus could make this wonderful promise. You can do nothing to lose what Jesus has promised you. You can't do anything to be unadopted by God. You can't do anything to be made into your old self again. There's no sin too big for God's mercy and grace. There's no limit to his forgiveness and love. You have nothing to fear. You are Jesus' and he is yours. Forever and ever and always.

▶ *Have you ever lost something important to you? How did that feel?*

CAN THOSE WHO TRUST JESUS LOSE THEIR SALVATION?   137

▶ How do you feel about the love, forgiveness, and salvation God has given you through Jesus?

1 — 2 — 3 — 4 — 5 — 6 — 7 — 8 — 9 — 10

NERVOUS   SAFE

▶ What questions do you have so far?

▶ What are you wondering about because of what you've heard?

PRAYER

God, thank you that when we trust in Jesus, you give us eternal life that can never be lost or taken from us. Amen.

FAMILY ACTIVITY: VISIT

Do it. Visit a national, state, or local park, preferably one with mountains, rivers, or some other impressive physical feature.

Discuss it. Talk about how many things in the world seem permanent—like what we see in nature—but they aren't really. These features can all wear down in various ways, and the world itself isn't permanent.

Connect it. Share that, unlike things around us that seem permanent, our relationship with God truly is permanent.

▼ JESUS CONNECTION ▼

Knowing we have eternal life no matter what shouldn't cause us to live however we want; instead, it should cause us to live with gratitude, joy, and a desire to obey God. Jesus sticks with us no matter what, through thick and thin. To live like Jesus means we do the same with God. We live in faith, fully committed to following Jesus.

▶ How can you live boldly for Jesus this week, knowing you are safe forever with him?

PART 6

THE BIBLE

THE STUDY OF THE BIBLE, an area of theology called *bibliology*, is somewhat unique from the other areas of theology in that it looks toward the Bible to understand what it says about itself. Some people would see this as circular reasoning and thus conclude it's problematic. After all, how reliable can what the Bible says about itself be? But this would be a problem only if the Bible were a normal book. That it most surely is not.

The word *bible* means "book," but the Bible isn't like any other book; it's in a class by itself. And the primary reason for that is because of who wrote the Bible: God. The Bible was given to us by God, who used human authors to record exactly what he wanted written down and preserved. And because God is faithful and true, and because he cannot lie or make a mistake, that requires that the Bible be faithful and true without any lies or mistakes. A perfect God cannot make something imperfect. This is why we can trust what the Bible says about itself. Ultimately, it isn't the Bible saying what is true about the Bible; it's God saying what is true about the Bible.

This section might surprise you as you get started. The first three questions don't really mention the Bible. That's because before we can explore understanding the Bible itself, we must understand the nature of revelation, the two primary ways we can know anything about God, one of which led to the Bible. All we know of God is what he has chosen to reveal to us. He hasn't just chosen what to reveal; he has chosen how to reveal it too. One way he has chosen to reveal information about himself is through creation, called *general revelation*. This is available to everyone; thus, the term *general*. The other way God has revealed himself is through the Bible, called *special revelation*. This special revelation is how we can know the most about God and how we can come to know him personally. It's how we can have a relationship with him through Jesus. This is why the Bible is so important. Without it we would have no way to know what Jesus has done to provide forgiveness of sin and how we can trust in him for forgiveness and eternal life.

As you walk through this section, be sure to celebrate the amazing gift God has given us in the Bible. Seek to help your child not just to understand the Bible, but also to love the Bible. But don't let the Bible be the final object of your child's love; let that be God, the author of the Bible, the glorious one whom the Bible is about.

62 CAN WE KNOW THE ONE TRUE GOD?

Yes. We can know the one true God because he wants us to know him, and he has revealed himself to us through general and special revelation.

HEBREWS 1:1-3 (OR 1:1)

One of the most amazing truths about God is that he made us to know him. He didn't just create us and then stand back in secret to watch us from afar. He created us and then showed himself to us so we can know who he is, what he is like, and how we can know him, love him, worship him, and obey him. This process of God showing himself to us is called *revelation*. To reveal something is to show something that was hidden or that wasn't seen before.

Think of playing hide-and-seek and not being able to find someone who then must reveal herself—to show where she was hiding. That's sort of what God has done. Because God is spirit, he has no body we can see. So he's revealed himself to us in ways we can see. And he's done that in two main ways: general revelation and special revelation. We'll talk more about each of these later, but for now, don't miss the simple beauty that you exist to know God and be known by God!

At times God might seem distant and confusing to you, but he doesn't have to be. And he surely doesn't want to be. In fact, he's chasing after you! Don't believe that? That's what the writer of Hebrews tells us at the start of his book. God has been chasing after people in many ways so they can come to know him, and the greatest of these ways is through Jesus. When you stop and look around, you'll see that God isn't as hard to find as you might think. His "fingerprints" are everywhere—each one placed intentionally by our loving God to draw us to him.

▶ *What questions do you have about God?*

CAN WE KNOW THE ONE TRUE GOD?

▶ How does it make you feel knowing that God wants to know you and for you to know him?

1 — 2 — 3 — 4 — 5 — 6 — 7 — 8 — 9 — 10

THAT'S OKAY   THAT'S AWESOME

▶ What questions do you have so far?

▶ What are you wondering about because of what you've heard?

PRAYER

God, thank you for revealing yourself to us even though you didn't have to. Amen.

FAMILY ACTIVITY: PLAY

Do it. Play Clue or Clue Junior.

Discuss it. Talk about how in the game you must do all the work to discover the criminal or the one who broke the toy.

Connect it. Share how God has done the opposite; he has done all the work to reveal himself to us.

▼ JESUS CONNECTION ▼

The best way we can know God is through Jesus because he is God. Jesus came to earth not only to provide salvation for us but also to show us God. And to do that, he spent time with people. To live like Jesus, we need to do the same. It's good to pursue friendships with others and show them Jesus!

▶ Who can you try to spend time with this week to get to know better?

63 CAN WE FULLY KNOW GOD?

While we can know much about God, we can't fully know him because of our limited minds.

JOB 36:26-33 (OR 36:26)

Think about how long a second is. No problem, right? Okay, now think about how long a minute is. It's perhaps a little more difficult, but not impossible. The same is true of thinking about a day, a week, a month, a year, or even a decade. But now try thinking about how long forever is. Think about time having no beginning or no ending. Just "always-ness." Can't do it, can you? That's because our minds don't work that way. We think in terms of time.

This is just one way we're reminded how much bigger God is than us and, because of that, how we can't fully understand him. God is outside of time. He has no physical body and there is no place where he isn't present. He is three Persons in one. These are difficult truths about God that we simply can't understand.

This is what Job needed to learn. When Job experienced incredible suffering, he couldn't figure out why. He hadn't done anything wrong, so all he could think of was that God had made a mistake. But God corrected Job by telling him he was wrong to think he could figure God all out. God is much bigger than we can grasp.

Try not to let this discourage you! While there are many parts of God we can't understand as much as we want, there are many more parts that we can understand. And the parts we can't understand remind us how amazing he is. God is not one of us. He's what is called *transcendent*—above and beyond what we can imagine. So, imagine the greatest things you can about God. And know he's even better than that!

▶ **What are some things you know for sure about God?**

CAN WE FULLY KNOW GOD?

▶ How much about God do you think you know?

1 — 2 — 3 — 4 — 5 — 6 — 7 — 8 — 9 — 10
NOTHING   EVERYTHING

▶ What questions do you have so far?

▶ What are you wondering about because of what you've heard?

PRAYER

God, thank you for being bigger than we can understand but for making a way we can know so much about you. Amen.

FAMILY ACTIVITY: VISIT

Do it. Visit a planetarium or an aquarium, or go online to research outer space or the ocean.

Discuss it. Talk about how little we know about the universe and the ocean. Explain that even if we don't know everything about something, we can still appreciate what we do know.

Connect it. Share how this is true of God too. We don't know everything about God, but we can delight in all that we do know.

▼ JESUS CONNECTION ▼

It takes faith to follow God when we don't know some things about him. But it also takes faith to follow God when we do know things. God can call us to do hard things. In those times, remember what Jesus did. He came to earth to do something very difficult, yet he did exactly what the Father wanted him to do. That's trust! We can live the same way.

▶ How can you live in faith this week, even if you don't know what God is doing?

64

WHAT IS GENERAL REVELATION?

General revelation is God using creation to show people that he exists.

PSALM 19:1-6 (OR 19:1)

Suppose you were stranded on a deserted island, and after hours of wandering through jungles full of nothing but trees, plants, and critters, you stumbled into a clearing with a giant jet airplane. Your initial thought would likely be, "I'm saved!" But you'd have another thought before that one—a thought you might not even remember having. Your first thought would be something along the lines of: "This big shiny object in front of me was made by humans!" Your brain would recognize that this plane didn't assemble itself. It was made by someone. It's too technical. Its design is too complicated. It's impossible that the elements of the plane just happened to come together in such a way as to make a functioning airplane. Again, you wouldn't have to think about this; you'd just know it.

That helps us understand how general revelation works. All those trees, plants, and animals that you passed along the way—along with the rest of our planet, solar system, and universe—help us recognize that creation is too technical and elaborate to be here by chance. Psalm 19 tells us that creation needs a Creator, and that Creator is God. We call God revealing himself to us in this way *general revelation* because it is available for all people to see and experience. General revelation tells us there is a God, but it doesn't really help us know who he is or what he wants from us. But God wants us to know those things—how much he loves us, why he made us, and how we can know him. So God revealed himself to us in another way too. We'll talk about that next time.

▶ *What are some of your favorite things in God's creation?*

WHAT IS GENERAL REVELATION? 145

▶ How easily can you see God's "fingerprints" around you each day?

1 — 2 — 3 — 4 — 5 — 6 — 7 — 8 — 9 — 10

WHAT FINGERPRINTS?   THEY'RE EVERYWHERE!

▶ What questions do you have so far?

▶ What are you wondering about because of what you've heard?

PRAYER

God, thank you for making such an amazing world and universe to show us you exist. Amen.

FAMILY ACTIVITY: EXPLORE

Do it. Enjoy God's creation by going on a nature walk, going to the park, or doing some other favorite outdoor activity.

Discuss it. Notice the big things in nature all around you as well as the little things and talk about how creative and amazing their designs are.

Connect it. Share how what you see—order, beauty, power, splendor—hints at what the Creator is like.

▼ JESUS CONNECTION ▼

Jesus was mostly outside in the Gospels. That's how people lived then; they farmed and fished. That's also why Jesus used so many examples from nature in his teaching. He used what the people knew to explain God to them. This helps teach us how to tell our friends and others about Jesus. Like Jesus, we can use what people know and love to help them come to know and love Jesus.

▶ What are some ways you can connect what your friends know and love to Jesus?

65

WHAT IS SPECIAL REVELATION?

Special revelation is God using the Bible to show people who he is.

PSALM 19:7-14 (OR 19:7)

Psalm 19:1-6 tells us about general revelation, which helps us know that God exists. General revelation tells us there is a God, a Creator, and some things about him. We can see that our planet was made perfectly to sustain life with the right combination of gasses in the air, water to drink, land to live on, food to eat, and gravity to keep us from floating away. Because our planet is the perfect distance from the sun, we don't freeze or burn up. This leaves no doubt that the earth's Creator is a master designer! But none of that tells us his name. It doesn't tell us about his love, mercy, or grace. It doesn't tell us what we are to do on this amazing planet he created. This is where the Bible comes in. And Psalm 19:7-14 tells us about that.

The Bible is how we learn all we need to know about God, why we exist, why the world is broken because of sin, how we can be forgiven of our sin, and how our amazing God will restore his creation to perfection one day. The Bible doesn't tell us everything we might want to know, but it does tell us everything we truly need to know. The Bible is called *special revelation* because, unlike general revelation, it's available only to those who pick it up and read it. God has given us a wonderful gift in the Bible!

▶ *What are some things you know about God because of the Bible?*

WHAT IS SPECIAL REVELATION? 147

▶ **How much of the Bible have you read?**

1 — 2 — 3 — 4 — 5 — 6 — 7 — 8 — 9 — 10

NONE OF IT — ALL OF IT

▶ **What questions do you have so far?**

▶ **What are you wondering about because of what you've heard?**

PRAYER

God, thank you for giving us such an amazing gift in the Bible so that from it we can learn all we need to know about you. Amen.

FAMILY ACTIVITY: GATHER

Do it. Invite another family over for dinner or dessert.

Discuss it. Ask your guests to share about their lives, especially things you don't know about them.

Connect it. Later, share how your gathering is like what God has done for us in giving us the Bible. The Bible helps us know God in ways we couldn't know him otherwise.

▼ JESUS CONNECTION ▼

Jesus is fully God, but he also became fully human when he came to earth. As a human, Jesus grew and learned, and one of the ways he did that was by studying God's Word. Jesus had only the Old Testament in his day, but he knew it, taught about it, and used it in his daily life. As we grow to live more like Jesus, we can do the same. We can use the Bible to guide how we live.

▶ *What can you read in the Bible this week?*

66 WHAT IS THE BIBLE?

The Bible is God's revelation of himself, his purposes, his requirements of us, and how we can have a relationship with him.

REVELATION 1:1-3 (OR 1:1)

When we look at the world, we can know there's a Creator. The wonders we see aren't here by chance; they were made and designed by someone. But studying the world won't ever tell us who that Creator is. That's where the Bible comes in. God gave us the Bible so we'd come to know who he is and what his purposes are. We learn about his nature and character. We learn what he has done, what he is doing, and what he will do. And we learn about why he made everything in the first place. We wouldn't know any of this without the Bible. That's what we see in Revelation 1. There would be no way for us to know of God's future plan unless he shared it with John, who then shared it with us.

While the Bible is mostly about God, it's not all about him. God also gave us the Bible to understand ourselves. Why did God make us and what does he require of us? What is our nature and character supposed to be like? We see that God made us as the most special part of creation and that he loves us and wants to be in a relationship with us. But we also see how we fall short of God's design and purpose on our own.

Thankfully, the Bible also tells us what God has done to fix everything. Apart from the Bible, we'd have no way of knowing the gospel and what God has done to restore our relationship with him and what we must do—place our faith in Jesus—to be right with him. This is why the Bible is such an amazing gift to us, one we should cherish, read, believe, and live out.

▶ *What has the Bible taught you about God or yourself?*

WHAT IS THE BIBLE?

▶ How do you usually feel about reading the Bible?

1 — 2 — 3 — 4 — 5 — 6 — 7 — 8 — 9 — 10
IT'S A CHORE   IT'S A GIFT

▶ What questions do you have so far?

▶ What are you wondering about because of what you've heard?

PRAYER

God, thank you for not leaving us to figure things out on our own but giving us the Bible instead so we can know what to do. Amen.

FAMILY ACTIVITY: EXPLORE

Do it. Go to a bookstore to look at the different Bibles, or invite families over and ask them to bring their Bibles.

Discuss it. Talk about the different English translations available, the different types of Bibles, and the different features in Bibles.

Connect it. Share how God has blessed us with many wonderful Bibles, but they are helpful only if we read them.

▼ JESUS CONNECTION ▼

Jesus taught about loving and honoring the Bible. He said he didn't come to do away with any part of the Bible, but rather he came to fulfill it. One important way we can live like Jesus is by loving and honoring the Bible like he did. We want to grow to see the Bible as the gift it is and as the source of knowing God and experiencing life at its best.

▶ What teaching of the Bible can you live out this week?

67

WHO WROTE THE BIBLE?

The Bible was written by people who were inspired by the Holy Spirit.

2 PETER 1:20-21 (OR 1:21)

Most books have one author. *The Cat in the Hat* was written by Dr. Seuss. *If You Give a Mouse a Cookie* was written by Laura Numeroff. Some books were written by two or three authors. But the Bible is different. It was written by about forty different people, including Moses, Samuel, David, Solomon, Isaiah, Luke, John, Peter, and Paul.

These writers were very different. They had different jobs, such as fisherman, shepherd, king, tax collector, doctor, and prophet. They wrote over a sixteen-hundred-year span from about 1500 BC to about AD 100. They wrote in three different languages: Hebrew, Aramaic, and Greek, and on three different continents: Asia, Africa, and Europe. They wrote from prisons, palaces, cities, the wilderness, and more. And yet, even though so many different people wrote in different times and places and in different languages and during different situations, the Bible tells one unified message about God loving us so much he saved us from sin through Jesus. That's because these forty people didn't write their portions of the Bible on their own. Rather, God inspired these writers to record what he wanted them to say.

That's what we see in 2 Peter 1:21. Each writer was carried along, or guided, by the Holy Spirit. The idea here is that the writers were moved to write what the Holy Spirit wanted them to write, much like how the wind moves a sailboat where it goes (the same phrase used in 2 Peter 1 is used of a boat in Acts 27:15). This is why it's true to say both that the Bible has about forty different human authors and that it has one author, the Holy Spirit.

▶ *What are some of your favorite books?*

WHO WROTE THE BIBLE?

▶ **How well do you understand how the Bible was written?**

1—2—3—4—5—6—7—8—9—10

IT'S REALLY MUDDY   IT'S CRYSTAL CLEAR

▶ **What questions do you have so far?**

▶ **What are you wondering about because of what you've heard?**

PRAYER

God, thank you for making sure that everything in the Bible is exactly what you want it to be by the Holy Spirit's guidance. Amen.

FAMILY ACTIVITY: CREATE

Do it. Write a short story. Consider working on it together as a team or assigning a different part to each person to see how well it matches up.

Discuss it. Either way you do it, discuss the challenges of writing even a simple short story with other people.

Connect it. Share how the Bible's amazing unity shows the Holy Spirit's guidance.

▼ JESUS CONNECTION ▼

While Jesus didn't write any of the Bible, his words are in it. Some Bibles put his words in red to make them easier to find. But that doesn't mean the red words are more important than the others. All the Bible is from the Holy Spirit and matters. That's how Jesus lived—no detail of the Bible and no command was any less important than the others. He obeyed the Bible, and so should we.

▶ *What command in the Bible can you be sure to obey this week?*

68

IS THE BIBLE TRUE?

Yes. Because the Bible is inspired by the Holy Spirit, it is true and without error.

2 TIMOTHY 3:16-17 (OR 3:16)

Have you ever seen a small child "help" an adult lift something heavy? The child might have placed his hands on the item and tried his hardest to lift it, but who really lifted it? The adult, right? The adult's strength is really what mattered the most. This might be a helpful picture when it comes to how the Holy Spirit guided the human authors to write the Bible. They had a role to play, but the Holy Spirit did the "heavy lifting." The partnership wasn't fifty-fifty, with the humans having as much input and control as the Holy Spirit.

That's at the heart of what Paul tells us in 2 Timothy 3:16. All Scripture is inspired by the Holy Spirit, and because the Holy Spirit is God, he is perfect and can't make any mistakes or lie. And because he gave us the Bible, we can be sure the Bible has no mistakes or lies in it. This is what it means when people say the Bible is *inerrant*. It is without error. We can trust the Bible completely!

Now, we have to be careful not to make this mean something it isn't supposed to mean. Inerrancy doesn't mean that every claim in the Bible is true. Take, for example, how in Genesis 3:4 the serpent told Eve she wouldn't die if she ate from the forbidden tree. This was a lie and we shouldn't believe it. Inerrancy doesn't mean that what the serpent said must be true; it means that the serpent's lie in Genesis 3:4 really happened. The Bible records that conversation between the serpent and Eve truthfully. The Bible is true and makes no errors in telling us how things really happened. That means we can trust the Bible!

▶ *What books or shows do you like that are make-believe?*

IS THE BIBLE TRUE?

▶ **How much do you believe the Bible is true?**

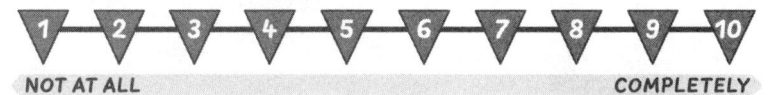

1 — 2 — 3 — 4 — 5 — 6 — 7 — 8 — 9 — 10

NOT AT ALL   COMPLETELY

▶ **What questions do you have so far?**

▶ **What are you wondering about because of what you've heard?**

PRAYER

God, thank you for always being true and giving us a Bible we can trust. Amen.

FAMILY ACTIVITY: EXPLORE

Do it. Go for a hike and show how a compass or compass app works.

Discuss it. Talk about how sometimes it's easy to get confused and think you're going the right direction when you aren't. But if you have a compass, it will always show true north and can be trusted to lead you the right way.

Connect it. Share how the Bible is our compass for life, always showing us the right way to live.

▼ JESUS CONNECTION ▼

Just like we can trust the Bible because it's God's words and his words are true, we can trust Jesus too. Jesus is God, so everything he said is true. Jesus never lied or misled anyone. As we try to live like Jesus, it's important that we be careful with our words. We can do our best not to lie or mislead anyone. We want every word we say to be true.

▶ **How can you be more careful with your words this week?**

69

WHAT IS THE BIBLE ABOUT?

The Bible tells us the true story of God providing Jesus to save us from our sin and how we can know, love, worship, and obey him.

LUKE 24:22-27 (OR 24:27)

Reading the Bible can be challenging. It's a big book of sixty-six smaller books totaling about 750,000 words. It's full of unusual names and places and describes events and cultures we often aren't that familiar with. But there's one thing that ties it all together: Jesus. That's what he told two travelers on the road to Emmaus in Luke 24. Understanding that the Bible is one big story about Jesus can be sort of a road map, reminding us where we are and where we're going as we read.

We can think of the Bible in six big parts:

- Part one is *God Creates* (Genesis 1-2), which describes how and why God made everything.
- Part two is *People Disobey* (Genesis 3), which explains how people sinned and messed everything up.
- Part three is *God Promises Jesus* (Genesis 4–Malachi), which traces how God began his rescue plan through Jesus.
- Part four is *God Provides Jesus* (Matthew–John), which describes Jesus coming to earth, living a perfect life, dying for sin, and rising from the dead.
- Part five is *Believers Obey* (Acts–Jude), which shares the difference Jesus makes in a person's life.
- And finally, part six is *God Recreates* (Revelation), which tells how Jesus will return one day to make everything right.

Understanding that the Bible is all about Jesus and how through him we can be forgiven of sin and live the way God made us to live can be a huge help. It won't make those hard names easier to pronounce or some of the stories less confusing, but it will help you remember why it all matters!

▶ *What is your favorite Bible story?*

WHAT IS THE BIBLE ABOUT?

▶ How clear is the Bible's one big story to you?

1 — 2 — 3 — 4 — 5 — 6 — 7 — 8 — 9 — 10
I'M SO LOST   I'VE GOT IT!

▶ What questions do you have so far?

▶ What are you wondering about because of what you've heard?

PRAYER

God, thank you for giving us such an amazing Bible that tells us how through Jesus we can be forgiven of our sins and know you. Amen.

FAMILY ACTIVITY: VISIT

Do it. Attend or watch a sporting event.

Discuss it. Talk about the different parts of the sport, such as the rules, what the athletes wear, the equipment used, and so forth. Explain that some of these things can be confusing at times, or they can often go unnoticed, but they all work together to make the sport work.

Connect it. Share that the Bible is like that—it all works together with one purpose of helping us see, believe in, and live like Jesus.

▼ JESUS CONNECTION ▼

All the Bible, even the Old Testament, is about Jesus. While we won't read the name *Jesus* in the Old Testament, that doesn't mean he isn't there. One of the ways we see Jesus in the Old Testament is through people who lived like Jesus even before he came. When they obeyed God's rules, they lived like Jesus! Ultimately, we don't copy those Old Testament people; we copy Jesus.

▶ What is one way you can live more like Jesus based on someone you've met in the Old Testament?

PART 7

CHRISTIAN LIVING

FAR TOO OFTEN, people can focus almost exclusively on the gospel leading up to the point of salvation. That's critical, of course. We want and need to present the gospel to a person so that he or she places faith in Jesus and is saved. But the problem is that there's far more to the gospel than that. If the act of salvation were our ultimate goal, then wouldn't it make sense for God to take us to our perfect home to be with him the instant we trust in Jesus? But he doesn't. He leaves us here on a broken earth. Why?

The reason is twofold. First, we're left here so God can use us to help others come to saving faith through Jesus too. Second, we're left here because God made us to do far more than just be saved. He created us to glorify him, love him, worship him, serve him, and obey him. That's our design. And when we do that, we experience the abundant living Jesus promised (John 10:10).

In this section, the longest one in The Family Catechism, we will explore an area called *practical theology*. It's just what it sounds like: theology that's practical or theology we can "touch."

This area is all about everyday, real-world, hands-on truths we can live out wherever we are as we do whatever we do. This section on practical theology can't stand alone, though. It makes sense only if it stands on the foundation of the doctrines that have come before it. We can't live the way God made us to live if we don't have our sin problem dealt with, and that can happen only through Jesus.

This is critical for us to stress as we walk through this section with our children. If we try to do what is covered in this section in our own power, we're going to fail and get frustrated. But when we trust in Jesus, he makes us new in him, and when we're relying on the Holy Spirit who's been given to us, we can live exactly how we were made to live. We won't be able to do this perfectly on this side of eternity, but we will find ourselves growing gradually to live more like Christ day by day.

As you cover the content in this section, raise a high bar! Don't let your family settle for less than God's best. But at the same time, be sure that grace and patience saturate your family as well. God calls us to live for him and expects us to do that. But he also lovingly comes alongside us to help us do what he expects of us, and he pours his limitless grace and mercy over us as we move, sometimes ploddingly, in that direction.

70 WHY SHOULD WE GLORIFY GOD?

We should glorify God, or celebrate him, because of who he is and because he made us, loves us, and takes care of us.

REVELATION 4:5-11 (OR 4:11)

In Revelation 4, John saw an amazing scene in heaven of twenty-four elders worshiping God by declaring that God is worthy to be glorified. You probably don't use the word *glorify* every day. In fact, this might be the first time you've ever heard it. So what does it mean? It means to celebrate or to magnify. This is where two tools you're probably familiar with can help.

First, there's a microscope, which makes something small seem big. The second tool is a telescope, which makes something far seem close. Putting these two tools together is how we glorify God. We glorify God by celebrating him and making him look more like he really is to others. People might think God is small and far away, but that's not true. When we glorify God, we show him like he really is: big and close!

There are many reasons why we should glorify God, but one of the main ones is because he made us. We wouldn't exist without God! We owe our lives to him, so we should want to glorify our Creator. Why God made us is another reason to glorify him. God made us so we could experience his amazing, never-ending love. We are the best thing God made and he placed us at the center of creation. Knowing this should cause us to want to put him at the center of our lives and show others how wonderful he is. A third reason we should glorify God is because he takes care of us. We would have nothing without him. Once again, when we are reminded how amazing God is to us, that should cause us to want to share how amazing he is with others. God is truly worthy of glory!

▶ *What makes you most want to celebrate God?*

WHY SHOULD WE GLORIFY GOD?

▶ **How big and close does God feel to you?**

1 — 2 — 3 — 4 — 5 — 6 — 7 — 8 — 9 — 10
NOT AT ALL   VERY MUCH SO

▶ **What questions do you have so far?**

▶ **What are you wondering about because of what you've heard?**

PRAYER

God, thank you for being worth celebrating every day because of who you are and what you have done. Amen.

FAMILY ACTIVITY: EXPERIMENT

Do it. Use a telescope, binoculars, or a phone's camera zoom feature to see things off in the distance.

Discuss it. Talk about how amazing the world God made is, including our eyes that we see with.

Connect it. Share that God has us here on earth to help others see how amazing he is. We're to be like a telescope or binoculars!

▼ JESUS CONNECTION ▼

While Jesus was on earth, he loved talking about the Father and showing others how wonderful he is. There was no doubt Jesus loved the Father and wanted to please him and glorify him, even when that meant Jesus had to do something difficult—like go to the cross. When we celebrate God, even in hard times, we live like Jesus.

▶ *How can you celebrate God this week, no matter what?*

71. HOW CAN WE GLORIFY GOD?

We can glorify God by loving him, worshiping him, and obeying him.

JOHN 15:8-11 (OR 15:8)

Our purpose on earth is to glorify God—to show others how amazing he is. But how exactly do we do that? It's easier than we might think. God designed us to glorify him! Just like God designed apple trees to produce apples, he designed people to produce fruit that glorifies him. That's what Jesus had in mind in John 15. So what is this fruit? We're made to love, trust, and obey God.

We love God not just by having loving feelings toward him but also by acting in love. We recognize that God is our greatest treasure and that everything else comes after him. God is our top priority in life. Others should see this about us, not because we're trying to show off, but because it's how we live each day.

This naturally leads to us worshiping God. When we love God, we'll find ways to celebrate that he's wonderful, dependable, and good. Of all the fantastic reasons to worship God, none is more fantastic than Jesus coming to earth, dying for our sins, and rising from the grave. Our worship might be singing to God, talking about God, or living for God. And that takes us to the third key way we glorify God—by obeying him.

When we obey God, it shows others that he is our Lord—our master—and that he's in charge of everything. We do what he says, even when it's difficult or unpleasant. One of the best ways we can obey God is by telling others about Jesus as he has sent us out to do.

When we think of glorifying God simply as loving, worshiping, and obeying him, we can do exactly what we were made to do. We can produce fruit that honors God!

▶ *Which do you like to do most: love God, worship God, or obey God?*

HOW CAN WE GLORIFY GOD?

▶ How good of a job do you think you do of glorifying God?

1 — 2 — 3 — 4 — 5 — 6 — 7 — 8 — 9 — 10

I'M PRETTY BAD AT IT   I'M AN EXPERT

▶ What questions do you have so far?

▶ What are you wondering about because of what you've heard?

PRAYER

God, thank you for being an amazing God worth glorifying. Amen.

FAMILY ACTIVITY: WORSHIP

Do it. Go to a place that helps your family connect with God. Spend time worshiping there. Sing, read the Bible, share together, enjoy a meal, or perhaps do this devotion there.

Discuss it. Talk about the ways you can glorify God in daily living.

Connect it. Share that the more we glorify God, the more natural it will become because it's what we are designed to do!

▼ JESUS CONNECTION ▼

Jesus was an expert at glorifying the Father. He loved the Father deeply, worshiped the Father fully, and obeyed the Father perfectly. We can't miss how Jesus spent time with others so they could see this. He knew that when others saw him glorify God, they'd want to know God. To live like Jesus is to do the same. We can spend time with others who need to know Jesus so they can meet him through the way we glorify God.

▶ Who can you spend time with this week?

72

HOW CAN WE LOVE GOD?

We can love God by living for him and by loving other people because he loves them.

MARK 12:28-34 (OR 12:30-31)

They say that love is a verb; it's an action. Love isn't just a warm feeling we have, although that can certainly be an important part of love. But the biggest part of love is what we do. That means when it comes to loving God, our loving feelings for him surely matter, but what matters even more is what we do because of those feelings. Or what we do even when those feelings seem small or distant. What are we talking about? How can we love God through what we do?

Jesus tells us that if we love him, we'll obey him. That's what he had in mind in Mark 12 when he said that the greatest commandment—the one that is most important of all—is that we love God with all our heart, soul, mind, and strength. But Jesus then talked about the second greatest commandment—the one that comes oh so close to that first one. Jesus said this second critical command is that we love our neighbor. This means that if we truly want to love God, we'll act on that love by loving other people. Or to put it another way, we can't not love others and say we love God. Why? Because God loves those other people just like he loves us! And if we love him, we will love what—or better yet *who*—he loves.

One of the best ways we can love God, then, is by caring for others. We can value others. We can help others. We can put others before ourselves. And most importantly, we can tell others about Jesus. When we do those things and more, we end up loving God.

▶ *Who are some people that you love most?*

HOW CAN WE LOVE GOD?

▶ How good are you at loving others?

1—2—3—4—5—6—7—8—9—10

I'M PRETTY BAD AT IT   I'M GREAT AT IT

▶ What questions do you have so far?

▶ What are you wondering about because of what you've heard?

PRAYER

God, thank you for loving us and loving every single person in the world. Amen.

FAMILY ACTIVITY: SERVE

Do it. Make care packages for people without a home in your area. Include essentials and a note telling the recipients they're loved by God. Distribute as many of the bags as possible; keep any remaining in your car for later use.

Discuss it. Talk about the needs of people in your community. Think of other ways you can help provide for their needs.

Connect it. Share that when we help people—even in small ways—we love them and we love God.

▼ JESUS CONNECTION ▼

There wasn't any doubt that Jesus loved others, because he was constantly serving them. He was always acting in loving ways. That's a key theme in the Gospel of Mark. It pictures Jesus as a servant, always on the move helping people. We can't do everything Jesus did for people, but we can copy his heart for people and his desire to do all he could for them.

▶ Who can you serve this week to show you love them?

73 WHAT IS WORSHIP?

Worship is celebrating the greatness of God.

PSALM 95:1-7 (OR 95:1)

Have you ever experienced something so amazing, so wonderful, so fantastic that you just had to tell someone about it? Maybe you got the perfect Christmas gift or you went on an unforgettable vacation. Maybe you ate an amazing dessert or you watched an unbelievable movie or sporting event. Or perhaps it was getting a top grade, learning a new skill or trick, winning a game for your team, or deciding to trust in Jesus. Whatever it was, it was just way too good to keep to yourself. So what did you do? You probably told as many people as you could! You might even have looked for people to share your news with. You might even have felt like you'd just pop if you couldn't find someone—anyone—to share your experience with.

That's sort of what it's like to worship God. Worship is finding joy like that, but an even deeper joy because of who our breathtaking God is and the amazing things he has done. Worship is letting that joy out of you in some way. It might be by singing or shouting like in Psalm 95:1. It might be smiling or laughing. It could be by reading, thinking, whispering, or even crying. It might be by yourself, with your friends, with your family, or with your church.

Worship is whatever you do to share with God and with others just how great God is and how much you love him. There's no right or wrong way to worship God—as long as it's true, from your heart, and focused on God. There's only one great God, but there are many ways to celebrate God's greatness!

▶ *What amazing things have you experienced?*

WHAT IS WORSHIP?

▶ **How well do you think you worship God?**

1 — 2 — 3 — 4 — 5 — 6 — 7 — 8 — 9 — 10

ZERO STARS · FIVE STARS

▶ **What questions do you have so far?**

▶ **What are you wondering about because of what you've heard?**

PRAYER

God, thank you for being an amazing God who is surely worth all our worship. Amen.

FAMILY ACTIVITY: WORSHIP

Do it. Create a "worship board." Use a dry erase board, chalkboard, or posterboard to record reasons to worship God and ways you experience his greatness. Keep markers or chalk nearby and encourage everyone to write (or draw) additional reasons throughout the week.

Discuss it. Talk about what is on your worship board and which reasons or ways mean the most to you.

Connect it. Share how we'll never run out of reasons to worship God because he is just that amazing!

▼ JESUS CONNECTION ▼

Jesus never missed a chance to celebrate the Father's greatness. He worshiped the Father when he was alone, when he was with friends, and when he was around tons of people. Jesus was busy, but he was never too busy to worship. As we grow to live more like Jesus, we can't miss worshiping God as part of our normal rhythm of life. More than that, we can't miss how amazing a gift worshiping God is!

▶ **How can you worship God this week?**

74

HOW CAN WE WORSHIP GOD?

We can worship God by making him our top priority in life and by being grateful to him for all we have.

ACTS 16:22-34 (OR 16:25)

Everyone worships. It's what we're wired to do. We might not call it worship or realize we do it, but we all have something—or several things—we love to celebrate and praise. Sports. School. Celebrities. Money. Art. Music. Family. Friends. Games. Clothes. There's nothing wrong with loving these things. And there's nothing wrong with sharing your love of them with others.

But sometimes, we make the mistake of going farther than that. We don't just love these things; we begin to worship them—to hold them up as the most important things in our lives. It's okay if they're important, but it's not okay if they're most important. That's God's spot. None of these things—as good as they might be—can come close to fulfilling us like God. None love us like God. None provide for us like God. And we don't owe our very lives to any of them. God alone deserves our worship!

We sometimes think of worship as what happens on Sundays or when we gather as a family like you're doing now. Those are surely times of worship, but worship is more than them. We are always to worship in everything we do. That doesn't mean we sing twenty-four hours a day, seven days a week. But that does mean that everything we do can be done remembering how wonderful God is—even when life is hard like it was for Paul and Silas in Acts 16. To worship God with our lives means we recognize and celebrate every good thing he gives us—and there's so much that he does! It might be difficult to worship like this at first, but in time you'll probably come to see that it's harder not to find reasons to worship God.

▶ *What are some things you love?*

▶ How easily do you find reasons to worship God?

1 — 2 — 3 — 4 — 5 — 6 — 7 — 8 — 9 — 10
I CAN'T FIND ANY   I CAN'T STOP FINDING THEM

▶ What questions do you have so far?

▶ What are you wondering about because of what you've heard?

PRAYER

God, thank you for being so good to us and giving us such great reasons to worship you. Amen.

FAMILY ACTIVITY: GATHER

Do it. Invite your pastor or a worship leader to dinner or dessert.

Discuss it. Ask your guest what worship means to them. Invite them to share any tips on how to worship in meaningful ways.

Connect it. Share how it's challenging to keep God as our top priority, but that's at the heart of worship. With the Holy Spirit's help, we can do that!

▼ JESUS CONNECTION ▼

There's no question that the Father was Jesus' top priority. The proof is that Jesus came to earth and obeyed the Father in everything. He even allowed himself to be arrested and crucified, putting God's will over everything. When we're tempted to drop God into second place, we can remember Jesus. Keeping the Father as his top priority wasn't easy for Jesus, but he did it, and with the Holy Spirit's help, we can too.

▶ *What are some things that compete for God's top spot that you need to address?*

75 WHEN CAN WE WORSHIP GOD?

We can worship God anytime and anywhere, by ourselves or with others.

MARK 15:33-39 (OR 15:38)

So much happened during Jesus' crucifixion that one important detail can be missed: the temple curtain. The temple had two curtains. The first was at its entrance. It could be seen by anyone and it kept everyone but the priests out. The second curtain was deeper inside the temple. It separated the holy place from the most holy place. Only the priests were allowed in the holy place to see this curtain and only the high priest could enter the most holy place, and only on the Day of Atonement.

When Jesus died, something amazing happened to one of those curtains—we don't know which it was. When Jesus gave up his life for our sins, the curtain was torn in two, from top to bottom. Why does that matter? Because it was a beautiful sign! Both curtains symbolized how people can't access God because of sin. But the instant Jesus paid for those sins, the curtain was torn, opening access to God. Don't miss how it tore: from the top to the bottom—from God down to people. Because of Jesus, all of us—not just the priests—can come before holy God!

This means we can worship God anytime, anywhere. We don't have to go to the temple in Jerusalem (it's no longer there anyway) or even our church buildings. There's nothing wrong with worshiping at church, but worship is too wonderful to do only a day or two a week. We can and we should worship all the time and everywhere.

Every breath you take is reason to worship God. Every blessing God gives is reason to worship him. Every hug from a family member or friend, good meal, beautiful sunset, favorite song or sport, the work we do, and much more are reasons to worship.

▶ *Where do you like to worship God, or where would you like to?*

WHEN CAN WE WORSHIP GOD?

▶ How often do you worship God?

1 — 2 — 3 — 4 — 5 — 6 — 7 — 8 — 9 — 10

HARDLY EVER   ALL THE TIME

▶ What questions do you have so far?

▶ What are you wondering about because of what you've heard?

PRAYER

God, thank you for providing the way to worship you all the time and everywhere. Amen.

FAMILY ACTIVITY: WORSHIP

Do it. Plan a day of worship. Think of the different ways and places you can worship God. Remember, worship should be a way of life, so it won't be all singing and praying. Consider how you can worship God in your regular activities.

Discuss it. Talk about how the day of worship went. What were the best parts?

Connect it. Share that each day can and should be like that day of worship.

▼ JESUS CONNECTION ▼

We can worship God anytime anywhere because of Jesus' sacrifice. Jesus paid the penalty for our sins, providing the way for God to accept us fully and finally. Sometimes it's hard to worship God. When you'd rather do something else, you don't feel like it, or you're distracted, remember Jesus' sacrifice for you and choose to sacrifice for him. You won't lay down your life physically like Jesus did, but you can lay down your desires for him.

▶ How can you remove whatever gets in the way of your worship?

76

HOW CAN WE OBEY GOD?

We can obey God by remembering that he is always faithful and that everything he tells us to do is for his glory and our good.

1 SAMUEL 15:1-22 (OR 15:22)

God had been so clear with King Saul. God was going to give the Israelites a big victory over the Amalekites, but instead of Saul and his army getting to keep some possessions as a reward like normal, God wanted them to destroy everything.

It wasn't surprising when the battle went just like God said it would go and the Israelites won. But when the prophet Samuel came afterward to check on things, he heard a surprising noise: the sounds of sheep and cattle! When he asked Saul why he hadn't destroyed them like God had instructed, Saul explained that these were the best of the flocks and that he and the soldiers were planning to sacrifice them to God. Was God pleased with Saul's plans? Not at all. In fact, God was so displeased by Saul's disobedience that he took the kingdom of Israel away from him. There's never a reason to disobey God.

Saul did what we can do at times too—we can try to outthink God. Sacrificing the best animals in worship to God might have made sense to Saul, but that's not what God had told him to do. Instead, what pleases God is when we trust him and obey him, even when his commands don't make sense or when we come up with a "better" idea. God never makes mistakes. He never misses thinking of "better" ideas. Everything he tells us to do is always for his glory and our good. And there's no better way for us to go. When it comes to obeying God, we need to remember that God is always loving and faithful to us, so we can always be loving and faithful to him!

▶ *Which of God's commands are hardest for you to obey?*

▶ How do you feel about God's commands?

1 — 2 — 3 — 4 — 5 — 6 — 7 — 8 — 9 — 10

THEY'RE MEAN   THEY'RE GOOD

▶ What questions do you have so far?

▶ What are you wondering about because of what you've heard?

PRAYER

God, thank you that everything you tell us to do brings you glory and is for our good. Amen.

FAMILY ACTIVITY: CREATE

Do it. Assemble a model, a LEGO set, a piece of furniture, or something else with detailed step-by-step directions.

Discuss it. As you work, talk about how important it is to follow the directions, even if they don't make sense at the time.

Connect it. Share how this is a picture of why we need to obey God fully and exactly, even if we don't understand what he's doing.

▼ JESUS CONNECTION ▼

Before Jesus was arrested, anticipating what was going to happen, he prayed, asking for another way. But Jesus also said that he would rather go through something difficult that pleased the Father than have something easy that didn't. It's okay when we tell God we're anxious or unhappy or confused by his commands. But then, we can copy Jesus and want only what pleases God.

▶ What can you do this week when it's hard to obey God?

77 WHAT SHOULD OUR ATTITUDE BE AS WE OBEY GOD?

We should obey God with thankfulness, eagerness, and joy.

2 SAMUEL 6:11-22 (OR 6:12, 14-15)

The ark was a piece of furniture in the tabernacle. It was different from Noah's ark; that was a big boat. This ark was a gold-plated box that held the tablets the Ten Commandments were written on. On top of the ark was a special gold lid with sculptures of two angelic creatures. When the ark was moved, it was carried by two poles slid through rings on its side. When the tabernacle was set up, the ark was placed in the most holy place—the innermost room of the tabernacle where God's presence was.

When David became king of Israel, he made Jerusalem the Israelites' new place of worship. That meant the ark had to be moved. As it was being carried to its new home, David was so happy, he couldn't help but leap and dance for joy. But when his wife saw this, she told him he should behave more like a king. David answered that he couldn't help himself—God was too good for him to contain his joy. This is how we should obey God: with overflowing joy.

Joy protects our hearts. When we lack it, we can become frustrated, angry, and selfish. But joy helps us be content in any situation—even ones that are difficult. We can have this joy by remembering that God is always good and that everything he does is for his glory and our good. It might not seem like it or feel like it at times, but that doesn't mean it's untrue!

This is why trust and joy go hand in hand. Trust feeds joy and joy reveals trust. As we discover God's will, the best thing we can do is trust God with joyful hearts as we submit to whatever his will is.

▶ *What makes you the most joyful?*

WHAT SHOULD OUR ATTITUDE BE AS WE OBEY GOD?

▶ How do you tend to feel when you obey God?

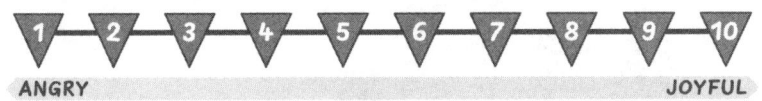

1 — 2 — 3 — 4 — 5 — 6 — 7 — 8 — 9 — 10

ANGRY   JOYFUL

▶ What questions do you have so far?

▶ What are you wondering about because of what you've heard?

PRAYER

God, thank you for giving us so many reasons to be joyful, most of all Jesus. Amen.

FAMILY ACTIVITY: VISIT

Do it. Go to a comedy show, watch a funny movie, tell jokes to each other, or do something else that gives your family joy.

Discuss it. Talk about how joy, happiness, and laughter are wonderful gifts from God.

Connect it. Share how we can be joyful even when life is difficult because God is always with us.

▼ JESUS CONNECTION ▼

The writer of Hebrews tells us that even though the cross was very difficult for Jesus, he obeyed the Father with joy (Hebrews 12:2). It wasn't suffering on the cross that gave Jesus joy; it was obeying and pleasing the Father. When we have a hard time obeying God with joy, it's helpful to remember Jesus' attitude as he went to the cross. He found joy in obeying God, and we can too.

▶ What can you do this week to be more joyful?

78 WILL WE OBEY GOD FULLY DURING OUR LIFETIME?

No. Because of sin, we are unable to obey God fully during our lifetime, but we can strive to obey him more each day.

ROMANS 12:1-2 (OR 12:2)

Did you know that if you wanted to walk a mile and walked halfway, stopped, walked halfway of what was left, stopped, and kept doing that, you'd walk forever but never walk a mile? That's because you'd always have a little more to go, even as it got smaller and smaller. You'd be so close, but you'd never cross the finish line!

Obeying God is sort of like that. The first step is wanting to obey God. The second step is actually obeying God. Sometimes this can be easy, especially when our hearts are right and we want to obey. But at other times—even when we want to obey God—this can be difficult. There will be times when we want to obey God but we don't because our sin keeps us from obeying. We may want to give some of our birthday money as an offering, but we think of the new clothes we could buy with it and we don't give. Or we might want to tell the truth about forgetting to feed the dogs, but we think about how we would have to stop playing our game to feed them, so we lie. We might try and try, but we'll never quite get there.

That's the bad news. But there's good news. Romans 12:2 tells us that God wants to change us to obey him more. As we grow closer to God and love and trust him more, we'll obey him more too. Instead of focusing on the amount left over—what we can't quite do to obey God fully—it's better to turn around and look at how far we've come! We won't obey God fully, but we'll see that we obey him more than we did before.

▶ What are some ways you've obeyed God recently?

WILL WE OBEY GOD FULLY DURING OUR LIFETIME?

▶ How do you feel about how well you obey God?

1 — 2 — 3 — 4 — 5 — 6 — 7 — 8 — 9 — 10

SAD AND FRUSTRATED   HAPPY AND MOTIVATED

▶ What questions do you have so far?

▶ What are you wondering about because of what you've heard?

PRAYER

God, thank you for loving us and being patient with us even when we struggle to obey you. Amen.

FAMILY ACTIVITY: EXPERIMENT

Do it. If you are able, do planks, sit-ups, or some other exercise. Take turns doing the exercise in silence. Then, do a second round as you encourage, clap, and cheer for one another.

Discuss it. Talk about the difference it makes to have people cheering us on and how we can do the same to help each other obey God more.

Connect it. Share how being part of a family and a church is looking for ways to encourage and motivate one another.

▼ JESUS CONNECTION ▼

Jesus never disobeyed, not even once. But that doesn't mean he doesn't know how difficult it can be for us to obey God. He understands temptation—remember, the devil tempted him to disobey the Father. The key for Jesus' obedience, and for ours, is to go a day at a time—even minute by minute. We can't worry about obeying tomorrow or next week; it's better to focus on obeying God right now in whatever we're doing.

▶ How can you obey God right now in whatever you're doing?

79

WHAT HELPS US OBEY GOD?

God helps us obey him by giving us the Holy Spirit, who helps us make choices that please and honor him.

JOHN 16:12-16 (OR 16:13)

Each day we make dozens—maybe even hundreds—of choices. Many might not seem to matter much—like if we want a hamburger or hot dog for lunch. But many matter quite a bit because they are choices of whether we will obey God. Some of these choices are clear and perhaps even easy. Others are confusing and difficult. Still other choices are challenging because they aren't about sinning or not sinning, or obeying or not obeying, but rather about what's best for us to do. Do we give a $20 gift to our church, to a homeless shelter, or to a refugee ministry? There really isn't a right answer to that question, but what we do matters and we want to do what's best.

Thankfully, the ever-present Holy Spirit is one of the many good gifts God the Father gives us. The Holy Spirit is God, so he knows everything. And because he's God, he loves us completely and wants what's best for us. So when we are faced with a decision between doing something that's right—that obeys God—or something that's wrong—that disobeys God—the Holy Spirit is right there with us to help us and guide us to obey. He will remind us that God is always good and loving and obeying God always is best. And when there doesn't seem to be a right and wrong choice, the Holy Spirit will help us make the best choice. With the Holy Spirit's help, every decision you make can be the one that most honors and pleases God.

▶ *What hard choices have you made?*

WHAT HELPS US OBEY GOD?

▶ *How good are you at making choices?*

1—2—3—4—5—6—7—8—9—10
REALLY BAD   REALLY GREAT

▶ *What questions do you have so far?*

▶ *What are you wondering about because of what you've heard?*

PRAYER

God, thank you for giving us the Holy Spirit to be with us and help us make choices that honor you. Amen.

FAMILY ACTIVITY: VISIT

Do it. Go to a buffet, a paint store, or some other place where you have plenty of choices to make.

Discuss it. Talk about how these decisions don't really matter for the long term, but every day we make other choices that do. Talk about how some of these big choices are easy, some are hard, and others might even seem impossible.

Connect it. Share that the Holy Spirit is with us to help us make choices that honor God.

▼ JESUS CONNECTION ▼

Jesus made choices—big ones and small ones—every day. And just like he helps us, the Holy Spirit helped Jesus too. As we try to make decisions that please God each day, it's important for us to remember that we can't do it on our own. We weren't meant to. Jesus got help from the Holy Spirit, and we can live like him and do the same.

▶ *What can the Holy Spirit help you with this week?*

80 WHERE DO ALL BLESSINGS COME FROM?

All blessings ultimately come from God.

JAMES 1:17-18 (OR 1:17)

Have you ever wondered where things come from? Take the food in your kitchen for example. Where did that box of breakfast cereal come from? Yes, it came from the grocery store, but what about before that? Well, it probably came off a truck through the store's loading dock, but what about before that? That truck brought it from a factory, and that factory got the ingredients off trucks through its loading dock. And those trucks brought those ingredients from other factories and wheat, corn, or rice farms. But we can't forget about the box and packaging! That's a whole other story. You can see that there's much more to answering the question of where a box of cereal came from than just the grocery store. Things almost always have a bigger origin story than we realize.

But things actually get much simpler the farther back we trace them. That's because all the blessings we have in life—all the good provisions and gifts we have—ultimately come from God! That's what James 1:17 tells us. Thinking of that box of cereal, God provided the wheat, corn, or rice, and he provided the sun, rain, and nutrients in the ground it needed to grow. God provided the trees the box is made of, and he provided everything else.

God might choose to give us some of his good gifts through other people—just like he uses farmers, factory workers, truck drivers, and grocery store workers—but they aren't the true source of these blessings. God is. We should be grateful for these other people, for sure. But more than that, we should be grateful to our loving God who is so good to us.

▶ *What is your favorite cereal?*

WHERE DO ALL BLESSINGS COME FROM?

▶ How often do you remember that God has given you all the good things you have?

1—2—3—4—5—6—7—8—9—10
HARDLY EVER — ALL THE TIME

▶ What questions do you have so far?

▶ What are you wondering about because of what you've heard?

PRAYER

God, thank you for giving us so many good things. Amen.

FAMILY ACTIVITY: EXPLORE

Do it. Visit a farm or orchard. Learn about what is grown or raised there and the work required. If you can, purchase some items (or if not, stop at a grocery store on the way home), and work together to make a meal or dessert using those ingredients.

Discuss it. Talk about the different sources of our food, clothing, furniture, and other household items.

Connect it. Share how God is the giver of all these good gifts.

▼ JESUS CONNECTION ▼

Jesus said that the Father is the one who gives us the good things we have (Matthew 7:11). Jesus wants us to recognize how good the Father is and to appreciate what he's given us. Even more than that, though, Jesus wants us to share what we've been given. That's true of Jesus himself too! Jesus is the best gift we've been given and we can share his love and tell others about him as often as we can.

▶ Who can you share some of God's blessings with?

81 HOW HAS GOD BLESSED US?

God has blessed us with life, talents, possessions, and, most importantly, salvation through Jesus.

JEREMIAH 29:10-14 (OR 29:11)

When we think of God's blessings, we probably think first of possessions—a home, clothes, food, toys and games, books, and things like that. While all these are indeed blessings from God, they aren't the only blessings God gives. Each new day is a blessing from God that we did nothing to earn or deserve. Our talents and skills are blessings from God too. If you're good at music, art, a sport, school, telling jokes, cooking, or anything else, it's because God blessed you with that ability. Sure, you've probably worked hard and practiced that skill or talent, but ultimately, your abilities come from God. But the most wonderful blessing God gives is forgiveness of sin through Jesus. God's other blessings might come and go, but this one lasts forever.

The forever blessing of God's presence is what he wanted his people to remember when they went into foreign captivity. Because of their sins, God's people were conquered by a mighty army and most of the people were forced from their homes and had to go to another land where they were held as captives. They might have lost most of the blessings God had given them up to that point, but they hadn't lost their greatest blessing: him. God would be with them even in Babylonia, and he would continue to care for them there. All God was doing, as difficult as it was, had a good purpose. Even the hardship they faced as captives was ultimately a blessing from God.

Sometimes God's wonderful blessings are hard to spot. But one blessing that is never hard to recognize is the gift of Jesus. No matter what other blessings we might or might not have, we can know with total confidence that Jesus is always with us!

▶ *What are some of your favorite blessings from God?*

HOW HAS GOD BLESSED US?

▶ How would you feel if you lost most of the blessings God has given you?

1 — 2 — 3 — 4 — 5 — 6 — 7 — 8 — 9 — 10
CRUSHED   FINE

▶ What questions do you have so far?

▶ What are you wondering about because of what you've heard?

PRAYER

God, thank you for giving us so many different blessings, but above all, thank you for the blessing of Jesus. Amen.

FAMILY ACTIVITY: CREATE

Do it. Hold a talent show, perhaps with some other families you know. Give each person an opportunity to share his or her talents. Create an award to give to each person who performs.

Discuss it. Talk about how our talents are part of what makes us special and how they all come from God.

Connect it. Share how we should be thankful for whatever blessing God gives us and we can use whatever it is for his glory.

▼ JESUS CONNECTION ▼

One way to respond to God giving us blessings is to be thankful. When we remember we don't deserve any of God's blessings, our focus can move away from being disappointed in what we don't have to being grateful for what we do have. Jesus taught us to be thankful for all God has given us—from the biggest blessings to the smallest ones—and that's what he modeled in his life.

▶ How can you let God know you're thankful for what he gives you this week?

82 WHO OWNS ALL THAT WE HAVE?

God owns all that we have and he trusts us with it as his stewards.

EXODUS 16:1-5; 17:1-7 (OR 16:4; 17:6)

When the Israelites left Egypt, they had to travel through a wilderness to reach the Promised Land. This wilderness was a place with very little water and where hardly any food grew. How would God's people survive this journey? Had God brought them out of captivity in Egypt just to die in the wilderness? That's what they thought. And so they grumbled and complained to Moses, their leader.

When God heard his people's complaints, he answered in an amazing way. He provided food and water for them, but that wasn't the amazing part. God loves his people and he wants to provide for them! What was amazing was *how* God provided for his people. First, he provided a mysterious food to eat called *manna*. If you go to a grocery store, you won't find manna on the shelves, because it isn't a food we have. It was a food God provided from heaven. Second, God provided water for his people to drink, but not from a river or a well. It didn't even come from rain. God gave his people water out of a rock!

God led his people into the wilderness without food or water and then he provided for them in these incredible ways because he wanted them to know he is the source of all they need. He wanted them to see that he loves them, he cares for them, and he can be trusted. God can bring food out of thin air and water from a rock because he owns everything and he is all-powerful. God gives us far beyond our needs. We can never forget that everything we have comes from our amazing, loving God.

▶ What's your favorite thing to eat or drink when you're very hungry or thirsty?

WHO OWNS ALL THAT WE HAVE?

▶ **How do you normally see your possessions?**

1 — 2 — 3 — 4 — 5 — 6 — 7 — 8 — 9 — 10

THEY'RE MINE   THEY'RE GOD'S

▶ **What questions do you have so far?**

▶ **What are you wondering about because of what you've heard?**

PRAYER

God, thank you for owning everything and for giving us what we need. Amen.

FAMILY ACTIVITY: CREATE

Do it. Bake two loaves of homemade bread. Take one loaf to a neighbor as a gift and enjoy the other one as a family.

Discuss it. Talk about how that bread and each of its ingredients belongs to God, as does everything you used to make it: your kitchen tools, your home, etc.

Connect it. Share that God created everything and he owns everything.

▼ JESUS CONNECTION ▼

Jesus was probably thinking about what happened to the Israelites in the wilderness when he said he was the bread of life and the living water. Just as we need bread and water to live, we need Jesus to have eternal life! And just like the Father provided manna and water to the Israelites in an amazing way, he sent us Jesus in an amazing way too. Jesus is our greatest possession, and like everything else, he was given to us by God.

▶ **How can you thank God for providing Jesus?**

83 WHAT DOES IT MEAN TO BE A STEWARD?

To be a steward is to take care of someone else's possessions and use them wisely.

MATTHEW 25:14-30 (OR 25:14)

In Matthew 25, Jesus told a parable—or a story—about what it means to be a steward. A man went on a journey and gave three of his servants some of his wealth. The first two servants took what they'd been given and earned more wealth for the man. But the third didn't. He did nothing at all with what he'd been given.

When the man returned from his journey, he asked for his wealth back. The first two servants gave back what they'd been given plus the extra they had earned. The man praised these two servants for being good stewards. They had done what he wanted them to do with what he gave them.

But the third servant gave the man only what the man had given him to start with. He hadn't lost any of it, but he hadn't added anything to it either. The man became quite angry. Why hadn't the servant at least put what he'd been given into the bank to earn a little interest? The man then punished this servant.

The point of Jesus' parable is that God gives us blessings in life. But God doesn't give blessings just for us to hold on to them, like the third servant. Instead, we're to be good stewards like the first two servants by putting everything God has given us to good use. God gives us gifts to enjoy and celebrate him. But he also wants us to put them to work. If we're going to be faithful stewards, we can't focus just on keeping what we've been given; we need to focus on using every single blessing to make God's glory known to all the nations.

▶ *What would you do with one million dollars?*

WHAT DOES IT MEAN TO BE A STEWARD?

▶ How do you use the blessings God gives you?

1 — 2 — 3 — 4 — 5 — 6 — 7 — 8 — 9 — 10
FOR MYSELF   FOR GOD AND OTHERS

▶ What questions do you have so far?

▶ What are you wondering about because of what you've heard?

PRAYER

God, thank you for trusting us as your stewards to enjoy and use the good gifts you have given us. Amen.

FAMILY ACTIVITY: SERVE

Do it. Clean out your home, garage, and storage and hold a family yard sale. Resist the urge to hold on to things you don't use much. Afterward, give part or all the proceeds from the sale to a charity.

Discuss it. Talk about how much God has blessed your family—so much so that it's hard to keep track of it all.

Connect it. Share how all we have can be used to glorify God.

▼ JESUS CONNECTION ▼

Jesus didn't have many possessions to steward, but he did have time and energy. Those are blessings from God too. Jesus used these blessings fully for the Father and for others. As we think of ways to live more like Jesus, we can learn about being good stewards of everything—our possessions and our time and energy—from him. Jesus put whatever he had to good use and so can we.

▶ How can you put your possessions, time, and energy to good use this week?

84

WHAT KIND OF STEWARDS SHOULD WE BE?

We should be stewards who take good care of God's possessions and who are generously and cheerfully ready to give them to others.

LUKE 10:25-37 (OR 10:33-35)

When Jesus talked about loving our neighbor, a religious leader asked who a neighbor was. This leader wasn't asking for Jesus' help to understand better. Rather, he wanted to find an excuse not to love people he didn't want to love. So Jesus told a parable—or a story—to answer.

Jesus said a man was traveling and was robbed and left injured alongside the road. Later, a priest came by but didn't help. A second religious leader did the same. But then a Samaritan came along. The Jews and the Samaritans didn't get along. But this Samaritan did something surprising. He stopped, helped the man, and took him to an inn. He gave the innkeeper money and told him to care for the injured man. If the innkeeper spent more than what he was given, the Samaritan would come back and pay whatever it was.

Jesus' point was that we are all neighbors—no one who should be beyond our love! That means we should be willing to use whatever God has given us to help others, no matter what. The key to being a good steward is having the right heart. When our hearts are focused on loving God and loving other people, we can be good stewards of God's blessings. We won't want to share just a little of our blessings with others to obey in the smallest possible way; we will want to share as much as we can.

This can be hard at first, but one of the best ways to develop the right heart is by doing it—practicing regular and generous giving. When you see the difference you can make in someone's life through your giving, it won't take long for cheerfulness in your heart to grow as you give even more.

▶ *If you could travel anywhere, where would you go?*

WHAT KIND OF STEWARDS SHOULD WE BE?

▶ Who do you normally see as your neighbor?

1 — 2 — 3 — 4 — 5 — 6 — 7 — 8 — 9 — 10
NO ONE   EVERYONE

▶ What questions do you have so far?

▶ What are you wondering about because of what you've heard?

PRAYER

God, thank you for giving us so many opportunities to love other people and provide for them through what you've given us. Amen.

FAMILY ACTIVITY: SERVE

Do it. Be a good steward of your time and energy by volunteering at a soup kitchen, a shelter, or some other local charity or ministry. If possible, try to establish a regular rhythm of serving.

Discuss it. Talk about your experience serving others. Was it hard? Rewarding?

Connect it. Share how this is how God wants us to live every day.

▼ JESUS CONNECTION ▼

The parable of the Good Samaritan is really about compassion. It's about seeing all people as valuable and loved by God and having compassion for them when they're in need. Jesus showed amazing compassion while he was on earth. Several times we read about his compassion for people—Jesus deeply loved people and did what he could to help them. As we look to live like Jesus, we can try to have compassion for everyone around us too.

▶ How will you be ready to help anyone in need this week?

85

WHAT IS PRAYER?

Prayer is talking with God as we celebrate him, share our needs and desires with him, and confess our sins to him.

LUKE 11:1-4 (OR 11:2-4)

We usually think of prayer as us talking to God. But that's only half the story. God also wants to talk to us! So it's best to understand prayer as talking *with* God. That doesn't necessarily mean God will talk to us with a voice we hear with our ears. But we can be sure that in prayer, the Holy Spirit will bring God's truths to our minds and stir our hearts to follow him.

Knowing that prayer is a two-way conversation reminds us how essential it is in our relationship with God. That's why Jesus prayed and why he taught his followers to pray. Our relationships with others wouldn't be healthy if we never talked with them, would they? The same is true of prayer. To grow closer to God means we'll talk with him often. But prayer isn't a chore or something we must do. It's a joy and privilege! It's not hard to talk with our friends, right? And we have no better friend than God!

So what can we talk about with God? Well, asking God for things is where most people start. We should ask God for what we need and want, but there's much more than that. We can also celebrate God and thank him for who he is, what he's done, and what he's promised to do. That's a big part of what we're designed to do! At the same time, we can also confess our sins to God, agreeing with him that what we've done is wrong, doesn't glorify him, and hurts us and others. This is where listening in prayer is so important. In these times of confession, the Holy Spirit reminds us that thanks to Jesus we've been forgiven and we're always loved by God.

▶ *Who do you like talking with?*

WHAT IS PRAYER?

▶ *How often do you try to listen to God when you pray?*

1—2—3—4—5—6—7—8—9—10
NEVER   ALWAYS

▶ *What questions do you have so far?*

▶ *What are you wondering about because of what you've heard?*

PRAYER

God, thank you for always listening to us and always wanting to talk with us. Amen.

FAMILY ACTIVITY: GATHER

Do it. Make a phone call or a video call to reconnect with family or friends you haven't talked to lately.

Discuss it. Talk about how good it is to connect with people you know and love.

Connect it. Share how wonderful it is that we can talk with God and that he always wants to talk with us.

▼ JESUS CONNECTION ▼

While Jesus was on earth, he often went off by himself to pray. Prayer was important for Jesus, and it was easy for those around him to see that. This is why the disciples asked Jesus to teach them how to pray. As we look to live more like Jesus, being people of prayer is a big step we can take. Like Jesus, make time to pray each day.

▶ *When will you pray next?*

86 WHEN CAN WE PRAY?

We can pray anywhere, anytime, for anything.

LUKE 18:1-8 (OR 18:1)

Have you ever interrupted someone? Perhaps that person was on the phone, talking with someone, or deep in thought. You likely didn't mean to disturb them, and you might have felt bad when you realized you did. Sometimes we think like that when it comes to prayer. We can be shy to pray because we think God is way too busy or what we want to talk about is not important enough.

But God is never bothered when we pray! He is always pleased to hear from us when we pray. That means there is no "right time" to pray. Anytime is the best time!

That's why Jesus told a parable—or a story—of the widow who wouldn't stop asking a judge for justice. In time, the judge finally gave her what she wanted. The point isn't that God is like the judge; it's that he's better than the judge. If even an uncaring judge will listen after a while, won't our God who loves us and always wants to hear from us listen right away?

In the same way, there aren't any "right places" to pray, although there's nothing wrong with having a regular time of prayer in a favorite place. The point is that prayer is never limited to any time or place. Furthermore, there's nothing too big or too small to pray about. If it's important enough for us to want to talk with God about it, it's even more important to him!

Remember, you never bother God when you pray. When you feel like praying about anything—even something that seems small and unimportant compared to what others are facing—that's exactly what you should do: pray about it. Our loving God is ready, willing, and able to listen.

▶ When is it hard for you to talk with others?

WHEN CAN WE PRAY?

▶ How much do you think God wants to hear from you?

1 — 2 — 3 — 4 — 5 — 6 — 7 — 8 — 9 — 10

HE WANTS TO HEAR NOTHING   HE WANTS TO HEAR EVERYTHING

▶ What questions do you have so far?

▶ What are you wondering about because of what you've heard?

PRAYER

God, thank you for hearing us all the time no matter where we are. Amen.

FAMILY ACTIVITY: VISIT

Do it. Go in the middle of the night to a restaurant or store that's open twenty-four hours.

Discuss it. Talk about why it might be open all the time, who might go there and why, and what it would be like to work a night shift.

Connect it. Share that places that are open twenty-four hours are more for our convenience, but God is always available to us because he loves us.

▼ JESUS CONNECTION ▼

Just like Jesus knew he could always talk with the Father, Jesus wanted others to feel that way about him. That's why when Jesus was disturbed, he didn't get upset. Instead, he welcomed whoever it was, whenever it was. This reminds us of Jesus' humility and love for people. As we grow to be more like Jesus, we can try to be just as humble and loving and never to see others as a bother.

▶ *What can you do to help you welcome anyone at anytime?*

PART 8

THE CHURCH AND LAST THINGS

PERHAPS ONE OF THE MOST startling statements God made in the Bible is what he told Adam in Eden, that it wasn't good for him to be alone (Genesis 2:18). It's jarring, really. On the heels of the refrain "it was good" that courses throughout Genesis 1, God deems something not good. And that should stop us in our tracks. Adam had God, of course, but God had more in mind for Adam. God knew Adam needed a companion.

In Genesis 2, we see that God hardwired us for relationship, primarily with him but with each other too. And while that often manifests in the form of marriage and family, God has given us another crucial relationship in the church, a relationship all believers partake in.

When we think of the church, we can think of it in two ways. First, it's all believers of all time. This is often called the universal or invisible church. Second, the church is the believers in one specific time and place who gather regularly. This is called the local or visible church. The church isn't perfect, but Jesus died for the church, loves the church, and is returning for the church one day.

In this final section, we'll consider the doctrine of the church, a field called *ecclesiology*, and the doctrine of Jesus' return or of last things, an area of study called *eschatology*. These two doctrines are tightly intertwined. The church exists to complete the mission Jesus began two thousand years ago as we wait for his return. What started out as a handful of believing Jews in and around Jerusalem has spread around the world, but as long as the sun rises in the east and there are people who haven't trusted in Christ, we have work to do.

That work will end one day, though. One day—no one knows when it will be—Jesus will return to earth. The first time he came as the suffering servant; when he returns, he will come as the conquering king. And on that day, Jesus will end all that is wrong. Sin, rebellion, suffering, and death will be no more. He will repair and restore everything that sin broke. Every wrong will be made right. This is a great day of hope—but only for those who have trusted in Jesus, his church. For all others, this will be a day of great mourning. Our calling is to follow Christ's guidance to do whatever we can to make that latter group as small as possible—prayerfully non-existent.

As you walk through this final section, be sure to cast a two-way vision to your family. The return of Jesus fills us with great hope, but it should also compel us to live out the mission he gave us—while there is time.

87 WHAT IS THE CHURCH?

The church is all believers of all time, as well as each local community of Christians who gather regularly and work together to fulfill the church's mission.

EPHESIANS 2:14-22 (OR 2:19)

When we think of church, we often think of a building. We might hear someone say, "Come on. It's time to go to church." That means it's time for us to travel to a building that we call our church. At other times, though, we hear "church" and think of an activity. We might hear someone say, "Come on. It's time for church." That means it's time to gather with others for worship, Bible study, preaching, and the other things we do together.

There's nothing wrong with using church in either of these ways, but neither is the truest and best meaning of church. Church isn't a place or an event; it's a people. This is what Paul tells us in Ephesians 2.

In its broadest meaning, the church is all those who have believed in Jesus from when he was on earth, through today, and then on until he returns. There's one big church that keeps growing and growing! We might look different, speak different languages, live in different places, and not even all be alive at the same time, but we're still one church.

But in another sense, the church is a group of believers who regularly meet together. There are many churches like this. Some are large with tens of thousands of people, others are much smaller, perhaps with ten people. These churches are in different places, and they look and act somewhat differently. They might not believe the exact same things, but together they believe the most important things. And God uses all these individual churches that are part of the one big church to tell the world about Jesus.

▶ *What are your favorite things about your church?*

WHAT IS THE CHURCH?

▶ **How does it make you feel to be part of the one big church?**

1 — 2 — 3 — 4 — 5 — 6 — 7 — 8 — 9 — 10

SO WHAT?   WOW

▶ **What questions do you have so far?**

▶ **What are you wondering about because of what you've heard?**

PRAYER

God, thank you for bringing people from every nation, language, and ethnicity together as one big, amazing church. Amen.

FAMILY ACTIVITY: WORSHIP

Do it. Visit a church that is different from yours—perhaps one of a different tradition, ethnicity, or language.

Discuss it. Afterward, talk about the differences between your church and the one you visited.

Connect it. Share how diversity is a great strength of the one big church. Even though people who know, love, and follow Jesus can be quite different, we are all part of one huge amazing family.

▼ JESUS CONNECTION ▼

It's important to remember there's one big church. Jesus has saved people from all around the world who are very different, but they all have become one in his church. What we have in common is far more important than our differences. As we grow to live more like Jesus, loving and welcoming all people should be our desire.

▶ **Who is different from you in some way that you can try to spend time with this week?**

88 WHO IS HEAD OF THE CHURCH?

The head, or leader, of the church is Jesus.

COLOSSIANS 1:15-20 (OR 1:18)

Think for a minute about the human body. It has many parts, each doing something different and important. But these different parts don't do only what's best for them without worrying about the other parts. Imagine if one leg wanted to go one way and the other leg wanted to go another way! It's not hard to see how the parts of the human body are designed to work together for the good of the entire body.

But what determines how they work together? That would be the head, or the brain. The brain controls the legs, telling them to work together to move in the right direction. The legs don't tell the brain which way they want to go. It just doesn't work that way. The brain is in charge.

Colossians 1 uses the picture of a body for the church. Each person brings important abilities and gifts to the church. Each person is important, including you. But each person of the church doesn't do what he or she wants. Rather, we all are to work together as one, following what our head—Jesus—tells us to do. That's important because we can have different desires, ideas, and goals. But even when those desires, ideas, and goals are good, if they're different, that causes problems. Think back to the human body: if one leg wants to go left and the other wants to go right, that's a problem. The same is true in the church.

This is why it's important for everyone in the church to recognize that Jesus is our head and we do everything we can to humbly follow him. The church isn't about what *we* want or think is best; it's about what *Jesus* wants and knows is best.

▶ *What else works together like the human body?*

WHO IS HEAD OF THE CHURCH?

▶ Do you feel like you are an important part of your church?

1 — 2 — 3 — 4 — 5 — 6 — 7 — 8 — 9 — 10
NOT AT ALL   ABSOLUTELY

▶ What questions do you have so far?

▶ What are you wondering about because of what you've heard?

PRAYER

God, thank you that Jesus is the perfect leader of the church and that we can always trust him. Amen.

FAMILY ACTIVITY: PLAY

Do it. If you are able, engage in a physical activity like playing a sport, hiking, or exercising. If you are unable, view online videos of athletes competing.

Discuss it. Talk about how God made our bodies to work together and that they can do some pretty amazing things.

Connect it. Share how God designed the church and talk about the great things it can do when it follows Jesus.

▼ JESUS CONNECTION ▼

Sometimes people who are in charge become selfish and prideful. Instead of doing what's best for others, they do what's best for themselves. But not Jesus. He's the perfect leader because he always leads the church in love. He always does what brings God glory and what is for our good. As we look to live more like Jesus, we can lead others like he leads us. We can be humble leaders who care deeply about others.

▶ How can you lead others with love and humility?

89

WHAT LEADERS SERVE THE CHURCH UNDER JESUS?

The leaders who serve the church under Jesus are elders and deacons.

1 TIMOTHY 3:1-13 (OR 3:1, 8)

Jesus is the head, or the ultimate leader, of the church, but he has chosen other leaders to help guide and care for the church under his leadership. This is sort of like in Eden how God gave Adam and Eve authority over creation, but he still had ultimate authority (Genesis 1:26-28). That's what Jesus has done with elders and deacons in the church, which Paul talks about in 1 Timothy 3. While churches understand these roles a little differently and perhaps use different titles, most churches have elders and deacons in some form. Churches would have at least one main pastor, though.

In many churches, elders are those who help teach the gospel and protect what the church believes, called *doctrine*. Sometimes elders are called pastors; sometimes they're not. In some churches, all elders are pastors. In other churches, there might be some elders who are pastors and other elders who aren't. Some elders might preach and be on the church's pastoral staff team, but other elders might not preach or be on that team. One thing all elders have in common is that God has given them leadership authority under Jesus to protect the church and care for it. As is true for Jesus' leadership, elders are never to lead the church selfishly or pridefully. Instead, they too are to lead humbly and lovingly.

Meanwhile, in many churches, deacons are those who are called to serve the church in various ways. In some churches, deacons have some level of authority, like elders. In other churches, deacons don't have authority. Instead, they're seen more as servants or helpers. Even so, they still can be considered leaders because they provide an example for others to follow in how they humbly and lovingly do whatever is needed to help the church.

▶ *What do you think it's like to be a church leader?*

WHAT LEADERS SERVE THE CHURCH UNDER JESUS?

▶ How does it feel knowing Jesus has chosen leaders to teach you, serve you, and protect you?

1—2—3—4—5—6—7—8—9—10
NERVOUS — THANKFUL

▶ What questions do you have so far?

▶ What are you wondering about because of what you've heard?

PRAYER

God, thank you for giving us elders and deacons to help lead and serve the church. Amen.

FAMILY ACTIVITY: GATHER

Do it. Invite a pastor, elder, or deacon for dinner or dessert.

Discuss it. Ask your guest what it was like becoming a leader in the church. What's good about it? What's challenging about it? Pray for that leader.

Connect it. Share how God is good to give us church leaders who love us and serve us.

▼ JESUS CONNECTION ▼

Jesus is God, which means he doesn't need help. But from the start of his ministry on earth, he wanted a team around him—first his disciples and then elders and deacons in the church. This shows how important community is to him. Together is better! There's nothing wrong with wanting to be by yourself at times, but as you grow to be more like Jesus, don't miss the beauty and value of being part of a team.

▶ How can you include others in what you do this week?

90

WHAT IS THE MISSION OF THE CHURCH?

The mission of the church is to make disciples of all nations by the power of the Holy Spirit.

MATTHEW 28:18-20 (OR 28:19-20)

It's easy to think that following Jesus is all about our relationship with him. It's certainly true that our relationship with Jesus matters a lot and that God cares deeply for each of us. But it isn't true that following Jesus is *all* about that. Jesus has given us a mission to make disciples of all people everywhere—that's what Matthew 28 tells us.

There are billions of people in the world who haven't trusted in Jesus. Some haven't even heard of Jesus! It's good and important that we love God. It's good and important that we learn as much as we can from the Bible. But following Jesus is about more than that. God loves the people of the world, and he wants us to love them too. In fact, we can't really love God without loving other people. And the best way to love someone is to point them to Jesus!

Now, you might think that's a really big mission and you're not sure what difference you can make. But remember, a journey of hundreds of miles begins with a single step. The same is true of our mission to share Jesus with all the people in the world. We don't do that alone—we do it as part of the church, and we do it a step at a time. Small steps over and over lead to big things!

We also can't forget that we don't fulfill this mission in our power. The Holy Spirit leads us, guides us, and empowers us to fulfill this mission. If it feels like it's too big of a mission for you, that's okay. You aren't supposed to do it in your power. We do it together as part of the church in the power of the Holy Spirit.

▶ *What country would you most like to visit?*

WHAT IS THE MISSION OF THE CHURCH?

▶ **How does the mission Jesus gave us make you feel?**

1 — 2 — 3 — 4 — 5 — 6 — 7 — 8 — 9 — 10
OVERWHELMED — EXCITED

▶ **What questions do you have so far?**

▶ **What are you wondering about because of what you've heard?**

PRAYER

God, thank you for giving us such an amazing and important mission to be part of. Amen.

FAMILY ACTIVITY: EXPLORE

Do it. Research on the internet to learn about the church in another country.

Discuss it. Talk about what that church is like, how big it is, and what challenges it faces.

Connect it. Share that even though you probably have never met the believers in this country, we all work together as one big church to fulfill our mission.

▼ JESUS CONNECTION ▼

The mission Jesus gave to make disciples around the world didn't start with his followers. Jesus started it while he was on earth. Jesus came to earth and gave up his life and rose again to pay the punishment for sin, but he also set this mission in motion. He formed a small team of followers who went out and made more followers to begin the church. Telling someone about Jesus is living like Jesus!

▶ **Who can you tell about Jesus this week?**

91 HOW DO WE MAKE DISCIPLES?

We make disciples by telling others the gospel of Jesus as we show them the love of Jesus.

MATTHEW 9:35-38 (OR 9:35)

Have you ever taken part in show-and-tell? That's when you show others an item that's important to you as you tell them about it. Both parts are important. If you simply show something to your friends but don't say anything about it, they probably won't know what it is or why it matters. And just telling your friends about something often won't do it justice. For example, it's difficult to find the right words to describe a favorite postcard you were sent from a faraway country.

In the same way, it's best that we use a show-and-tell approach to making disciples. This is what Jesus modeled, as we see in Matthew 9. Jesus traveled all around showing that he is God and that he loves people. He performed amazing miracles, healed people, fed people, and befriended people. But he also told people about God's kingdom. He explained how people can be made right with God and what it looks like to live for God.

This is what Jesus wants us to do too. We might not be able to do the miracles Jesus did and we might not draw huge crowds, but we can show others what Jesus is like by imitating his love and other characteristics. And at the same time, we can tell others about how they can be forgiven of their sins through faith in Jesus. When we show people how much we love Jesus, how much we love them, and how much Jesus loves them, and when we tell them about who Jesus is, we can help them understand the gospel.

▶ What would you want to take to a show-and-tell?

HOW DO WE MAKE DISCIPLES?

▶ Which are you more comfortable doing?

1 — 2 — 3 — 4 — 5 — 6 — 7 — 8 — 9 — 10

SHOWING THE LOVE OF JESUS   TELLING ABOUT JESUS

▶ What questions do you have so far?

▶ What are you wondering about because of what you've heard?

PRAYER

God, thank you for sending Jesus to show and tell us how much you love us and how we can be forgiven of sin. Amen.

FAMILY ACTIVITY: VISIT

Do it. Go to a museum or, if that's not possible, a store.

Discuss it. As you walk through the museum or store, talk about how difficult it would be only to tell about the items in it. Note how seeing the items up close makes a big difference.

Connect it. Share how in the same way we need to show and tell others about Jesus.

▼ JESUS CONNECTION ▼

All along, Jesus knew he'd lay down his life for people. He also knew most people would reject him. And yet his love for the Father and for us was too great to keep him from going to the cross. As we show and tell about Jesus, many people won't want to hear about him. But we can follow in Jesus' footsteps and gently and lovingly keep showing and telling. If we love other people, what else can we do?

▶ How can you love someone who doesn't know Jesus?

92

WHAT IS THE GOSPEL?

The gospel is the good news of how we can be forgiven of sin through Jesus and how one day Jesus will bring about God's kingdom and restore all things.

1 CORINTHIANS 15:1-8 (OR 15:3-4)

The word *gospel* means "good news." We love good news, don't we? We love to hear good news and we love to share good news. Imagine that someone gave you a million dollars. Do you think you would keep that good news to yourself? Of course not! You'd probably tell everyone you knew the good news of what happened to you. That's sort of what Paul may have had in mind as he described the gospel in 1 Corinthians 15.

The truth is that we've been given something far, far greater than a million dollars. Jesus is the Son of God who came to earth, lived a perfect life, died for us, and rose from the dead, all to be our Rescuer. When we trust in Jesus, we're forgiven of all our sins and we start an amazing relationship with our loving God. The King of kings adopts us as his children. God gives us the ability to live the way he has always intended us to live—with purpose and with joy. Our gracious God gives us eternal life with him and all others who have trusted in Jesus.

And one day, Jesus will return, make all things right, and set up God's perfect forever kingdom. That's where we will live with him and others who have trusted in him as we experience nothing but good things forever and ever. That's not just good news, is it? It might be better to think of the gospel as *great* news instead!

This great news is why the church gathers and why we live to tell as many others as we can about what has happened to us in Jesus. We simply can't keep such great news to ourselves!

▶ What is the best news you've ever heard? Shared?

WHAT IS THE GOSPEL?

▶ How good do you think the gospel is?

1—2—3—4—5—6—7—8—9—10
IT'S OKAY   IT'S FANTASTIC

▶ What questions do you have so far?

▶ What are you wondering about because of what you've heard?

PRAYER

God, thank you for providing Jesus to give us such good news to hope in and to share with others. Amen.

FAMILY ACTIVITY: CREATE

Do it. Buy a print newspaper and flip through it, noticing the different sections and types of articles. Make your own newspaper describing the life of Jesus and the gospel.

Discuss it. Talk about how much of the news in the newspaper is good news and how much of it isn't.

Connect it. Share how God's good news has difficult parts, but it's truly good news. Sin isn't the focus of the gospel; forgiveness through Jesus is. And that's definitely great news!

▼ JESUS CONNECTION ▼

Jesus is the source of the good news we share (there would be no gospel without him), and he also modeled how to share it. Jesus wasn't ashamed of the gospel, but he was also gentle and loving as he shared it. He didn't shy away from talking about sin, but he did so with love. As we share the gospel, we must talk about sin, but like Jesus, we want to do that with gentleness and love.

▶ How can you be loving as you tell others about Jesus?

93 HOW MUCH OF THE WORLD DOES GOD WANT TO HEAR THE GOSPEL?

God wants the whole world—people from every nation, ethnic group, and language—to hear the gospel and trust in Jesus.

REVELATION 7:9-10 (OR 7:9)

In the Old Testament, the Israelites were God's chosen people (Deuteronomy 7:6). God chose them to be a special people and to love them, care for them, and provide for them. But God also wanted to use them. It would be through this people that God would bring the Rescuer into the world.

The problem for many of the Israelites was that they thought because they were God's special people, the Rescuer was only for them and they were God's only people. They thought God loved only them, cared only for them, and provided only for them. That wasn't true! The Rescuer is for everyone, and God loves, cares for, and provides for all people.

When the church formed, the early believers were close to making the same mistake. Many of the early Christians were Jews. When Samaritans and Gentiles began trusting in Jesus, those Jewish Christians weren't quite sure what to do. So the Holy Spirit helped them see that the gospel is for everyone! They were to be one big church, welcoming everyone.

God's heart is for all people to come to know him through Jesus. He had indeed chosen the Jews to be a special people, but that wasn't so they alone would have a relationship with him. They were supposed to be a light in a dark world to share about God with others. And that's what God has chosen the church to do now. God's eternal kingdom will be filled with people from every tribe and nation, just like we see in Revelation 7. No matter what language people speak, how much money they have, where they live, what their skin color is, or what they wear, God loves them. And he wants us to love them too.

▶ *What language would you want to learn?*

HOW MUCH OF THE WORLD DOES GOD WANT TO HEAR?   207

▶ How much of the world do you want to trust in Jesus?

1 — 2 — 3 — 4 — 5 — 6 — 7 — 8 — 9 — 10
JUST WHERE I LIVE   ALL OF IT

▶ What questions do you have so far?

▶ What are you wondering about because of what you've heard?

PRAYER

God, thank you for creating people with such amazing diversity and for loving us all 100 percent exactly the same. Amen.

FAMILY ACTIVITY: SERVE

Do it. Research unreached people groups at joshuaproject.net, peoplegroups.org, or pray1040.com. Based on what you learn, take any action you are able to take.

Discuss it. Talk about how people around the world are all valuable and need to know Jesus.

Connect it. Share how God is so good to help you come to know Jesus and how you can love others by helping them come to know Jesus too.

▼ JESUS CONNECTION ▼

There's no limit to Jesus' love, which he showed while he was on earth. Jesus spent time with Jews, Samaritans, and Gentiles. He made friends with people who were rejected by the rest of society. He wasn't afraid to be close to the sick, even those with horrible diseases. As we look to live like Jesus, this can be true of us too. Make sure that no one is beyond your love, respect, and friendship.

▶ Who is different from you that you can try to get to know better?

94. WHAT ORDINANCES HAS JESUS GIVEN THE CHURCH?

Jesus has given the church two ordinances, baptism and the Lord's Supper, that help us remember what he has done and that we belong to him.

LUKE 22:14-20 (OR 22:17, 19)

Ordinance is a big word with an easy meaning. An ordinance is an act Jesus gave the church to do. Jesus gave us two ordinances: baptism and the Lord's Supper (sometimes called *communion*). It's important that we understand that Jesus didn't suggest these two ordinances. He commanded them. If a church is going to be a church, it must practice baptism and the Lord's Supper. How often a church does each might be up for debate, but that a church does them isn't. Churches baptize and churches celebrate the Lord's Supper. It's just part of what they do.

The Lord's Supper is when a church drinks wine or juice and eats bread together, remembering how Jesus gave up his body and shed his blood so we could be forgiven of sin. This is what Jesus began in Luke 22. Baptism is a little more complicated. For many churches, that's the act of dipping a new believer under water. It's seen as a way for that believer to tell others he or she is following Jesus. Other churches might sprinkle water. Others might baptize infants to show they are part of a community of faith.

While churches practice the ordinances differently (some even have a third one, foot washing), the ordinances remind all churches of Jesus' death and resurrection. One of the things we need to understand and remember most about Jesus is that he gave up his life for us but didn't stay dead. He rose back to life! And that's what he provides for us: trusting in him is the only way to die to our sins and be raised to new life in Jesus. Each time you celebrate baptism and the Lord's Supper, remember this wonderful news!

▶ *Have you been baptized and participated in the Lord's Supper?*

WHAT ORDINANCES HAS JESUS GIVEN THE CHURCH?

▶ **How much of baptism and the Lord's Supper do you understand?**

1 — 2 — 3 — 4 — 5 — 6 — 7 — 8 — 9 — 10

THEY'RE A COMPLETE MYSTERY · · · THEY MAKE TOTAL SENSE

▶ **What questions do you have so far?**

▶ **What are you wondering about because of what you've heard?**

PRAYER

God, thank you for giving us two wonderful reminders of the great sacrifice Jesus made for us. Amen.

FAMILY ACTIVITY: GATHER

Do it. Ask to meet with a pastor or leader from your church to share more about baptism and the Lord's Supper. If possible, ask to see where baptisms take place and how the Lord's Supper is prepared.

Discuss it. Talk about your experiences with baptism and the Lord's Supper.

Connect it. Share how both these ordinances are wonderful pictures of what Jesus has done for us.

▼ JESUS CONNECTION ▼

Baptism and the Lord's Supper wouldn't exist if Jesus hadn't sacrificed himself for us. His death is at the center of what we remember during each. The world has never seen a greater sacrifice! While we can't match Jesus' sacrifice, we're called to be ready to sacrifice as much as we can for others. To live like Jesus is to lay down ourselves for the glory of God and for the good of others.

▶ **What sacrifices can you make this week to point others to Jesus' amazing sacrifice?**

95 WHAT IS THE HOPE OF THE CHURCH?

The hope of the church is the return of Jesus, when he comes back to earth to usher in the kingdom of God.

REVELATION 19:11-16 (OR 19:11)

When we talk about hope, we often mean something we wish for without knowing if it will come true. We might hope for a specific game or piece of clothing for Christmas, but we don't know if we'll get it. We might hope there isn't a pop quiz at school, but we don't know if one will be given.

The Bible uses *hope* differently. In the Bible, hope is a confident expectation that what our faithful God has promised will happen. Even when it doesn't seem like God's promises will come true, believers can continue to hope in those promises with confidence, expectation, and eagerness. Hope in the world is unsure; hope in God is sure!

God has given us many wonderful promises to hope in, but the greatest one of all is that Jesus will return one day and make all things new. This is what Revelation 19 describes. The Bible pictures Jesus coming the first time as a suffering servant (Isaiah 53). But when he returns, he will come back as a conquering king! The first time Jesus came, he did what was required to provide salvation for all who believe. The second time he comes, he will complete that salvation. When Jesus returns, he will make all wrongs right. He will repair all that is broken. He will put an end to all sin, suffering, and death once and for all.

This is the greatest hope of the church. It's not just what the church wishes would happen; it's what the church knows will happen. And it's what gives the church the courage and strength to get through whatever difficult things a day might hold. Today might be dark, but a brighter day is coming!

▶ *What are some things you hope for?*

WHAT IS THE HOPE OF THE CHURCH?

▶ How eager and excited are you for Jesus to return?

1 — 2 — 3 — 4 — 5 — 6 — 7 — 8 — 9 — 10

IT MAKES ME NERVOUS   I CAN'T WAIT

▶ What questions do you have so far?

▶ What are you wondering about because of what you've heard?

PRAYER

God, thank you for keeping all your promises, especially the promise that Jesus will return and make all things right. Amen.

FAMILY ACTIVITY: VISIT

Do it. Visit a place where you haven't been for a while—the longer the better.

Discuss it. Talk about what is the same and what has changed.

Connect it. Share that the world has changed in many ways since Jesus was last here, but one thing that has remained the same is his love for people.

▼ JESUS CONNECTION ▼

Bad things often happen that can make us wonder what Jesus is waiting on. Why doesn't he return now and end all those bad things? Because God is giving people more time to trust in Jesus and be saved before it's too late. As God is loving and patient, we can be too. We should tell others about Jesus with urgency, but we should be patient too, waiting for God to work in their hearts.

▶ Who hasn't trusted in Jesus that you can pray for?

96

WHAT IS THE KINGDOM OF GOD?

The kingdom of God is God's rule over all things, which will be made perfect when Jesus returns and repairs all that sin has broken.

PSALM 145:10-13 (OR 145:13)

Every king needs a kingdom; he needs a land and a people to rule over. Psalm 145 tells us that God, the great King, has the greatest kingdom of them all—the entire world and all the people of the world. In fact, God's kingdom goes beyond the world—the entire universe is his! God created it all, which means he's in charge of it all. Everything is part of God's matchless kingdom.

God rules over his kingdom in three ways. First, he rules generally over all things. Although many people don't recognize God as their King and therefore don't obey him, that doesn't mean God isn't truly the great King. He's King not because people allow him to be King; he's King because he's the all-powerful Creator. God hasn't lost any of his authority or power over the world, even if sin has broken that world.

Second, God rules specifically over all believers. Those of us who recognize God as King love him and seek to obey him. We won't do this perfectly, but we still try to serve our great King as his loving servants. And because God is such an amazing and loving King, he provides for us, cares for us, and forgives us when we disobey.

Third, God will rule perfectly over all creation when Jesus returns. Jesus will fix all that sin has broken. All unbelievers will be judged for their sins, and all believers will be with each other and with Jesus from that moment on. In God's eternal kingdom, he will reign fully and perfectly over everything. Sin and rebellion will be no more. Love, obedience, and joy will replace it forevermore. God's kingdom is incredible, and it's incredible that he has made us part of it!

▶ *What would you do if you were king for a day?*

WHAT IS THE KINGDOM OF GOD?

▶ How much do you obey and serve God as your King?

1 — 2 — 3 — 4 — 5 — 6 — 7 — 8 — 9 — 10

MAYBE A LITTLE   COMPLETELY

▶ What questions do you have so far?

▶ What are you wondering about because of what you've heard?

PRAYER

God, thank you for being a good, loving King and for including us as part of your perfect kingdom because of Jesus. Amen.

FAMILY ACTIVITY: SERVE

Do it. Find a way to serve your community: clean up trash, plant flowers at a school, volunteer, etc.

Discuss it. Talk about how what you're doing is important because it shows in some way—even a small one—what the world is supposed to be like and what it will be like when Jesus returns.

Connect it. Share how living like Jesus gives snapshots of God's kingdom to others.

▼ JESUS CONNECTION ▼

Only Jesus can fix everything sin has broken so God's kingdom will be perfect and complete. However, when we live like Jesus, we show others a picture of what God's coming kingdom will be like. When we live with love, humility, compassion, generosity, hospitality, forgiveness, obedience, and more, we show others what the world is supposed to be like and what it will be like one day.

▶ How can you live like Jesus this week to show what God's kingdom is like?

97 HOW CAN WE SHOW GOD'S KINGDOM TO THE BROKEN WORLD AROUND US?

We can show God's kingdom to the broken world around us by opposing sin, promoting justice, and defending the helpless.

JEREMIAH 29:4-7 (OR 29:7)

Not everyone recognizes God as the great King. Even Christians can fail to obey him sometimes. That means the world we live in isn't like it should be. At times it's nothing like it should be. Everyone should love God and everyone should love one another, but not everyone does. Everyone should live with kindness, but not everyone does. Everyone should live with generosity, but not everyone does. Everyone should live in justice, but not everyone does.

Instead, people sin against God and they sin against each other, and they often seem to get away with it. Sometimes sin is even celebrated and allowed to flourish, while living according to God's ways is criticized and punished. Basically, in many ways, the world is upside down from how it's supposed to be.

Sometimes we might want to respond to all that is wrong in the world with bitterness or hopelessness. We might want to fight back or give up. At other times, we choose to ignore it. But that's not what God has told us to do. Instead, he wants us to live in a way that shows what the coming kingdom of God will be like. He wants us to give a picture to those around us of how things should be.

That's what he told the Israelites to do in Jeremiah 29 when they were taken into captivity. God didn't tell them to fight for their freedom or sabotage the sinful nation they lived in. Instead, he told them to pray for that nation and to seek to do it good. That's how we are to live. Work to make the world become more like the kingdom of God. Take one small step at a time to help turn the upside-down world right side up.

▶ *What are some ways you see that the world is upside down?*

HOW CAN WE SHOW GOD'S KINGDOM?

▶ How do you usually respond when you see something wrong being done around you?

1 — 2 — 3 — 4 — 5 — 6 — 7 — 8 — 9 — 10
IGNORE IT   SHOW JESUS

▶ What questions do you have so far?

▶ What are you wondering about because of what you've heard?

PRAYER

God, thank you for calling us to live boldly for you with love as we show a broken world how it can find restoration through Jesus. Amen.

FAMILY ACTIVITY: SERVE

Do it. Research ministries or organizations in your area that focus on promoting justice and defending the helpless. Schedule a time to volunteer with one of these organizations, or consider organizing a yard sale, bake sale, or some other way to raise funds for it.

Discuss it. Talk about what the ministry or organization does and why it matters.

Connect it. Share how God is good to give us ministries and organizations that work to show what God's kingdom is like.

▼ JESUS CONNECTION ▼

Jesus could have fought back, and he would have won. But when the religious leaders opposed Jesus and the crowds called for him to be crucified, Jesus didn't fight back. Instead, he gave up his life, even for those who were against him. In this, he shows us how to respond to a world that's broken. We always stand firm on God's truth, but we always stand firm in love.

▶ *How can you stand firm on God's truth in love this week?*

98 WHEN WILL JESUS RETURN?

Jesus could return at any moment, according to God's perfect timing

1 THESSALONIANS 5:1-6 (OR 5:2)

Have you ever gone on an overnight trip? You probably knew the day and time when you were supposed to leave. That was important because it helped you know when to get ready. You knew when you had to pack, collect anything you wanted to take with you, go to the bathroom one last time, and do anything else needed to get ready for the trip.

Imagine, though, that you were told you were going to go on the greatest trip ever but you weren't told when that trip would be. You simply had to be ready to go on a moment's notice. What would you do? You'd likely pack a bag and have it ready to go, right? You wouldn't wait because you wouldn't want to miss out on that trip.

We know without a doubt that Jesus is returning. He promised it. But we don't know when it will be. That's why Paul says that Jesus will come like a thief—when no one knows. Many people have tried to predict when Jesus is returning, claiming they figured out some code or formula in the Bible. None of these predictions have come true, though. That's because there is no code or formula. Jesus even said no one knows except for the Father (Matthew 24:36). So there's just no way to know when Jesus will return until he returns. All we know is that the Father has chosen a time for Jesus to return. And that time will be perfect, just like when Jesus came to earth the first time (Galatians 4:4). Until then, we live with hope, always ready for Jesus to return as we continue to fulfill our mission of bringing glory to God as we wait.

▶ **What is your dream trip?**

WHEN WILL JESUS RETURN?

▶ How ready are you for Jesus' return?

1 — 2 — 3 — 4 — 5 — 6 — 7 — 8 — 9 — 10

NO, WAIT!   COME ON!

▶ What questions do you have so far?

▶ What are you wondering about because of what you've heard?

PRAYER

God, thank you for the promise that Jesus is coming back to earth at just the right time. Amen.

FAMILY ACTIVITY: CELEBRATE

Do it. Plan a fun family outing, but don't share what it is or when it will happen. Only let everyone know a surprise is coming. When the time is right, announce the surprise and enjoy the time as a family.

Discuss it. Talk about what it was like waiting for the outing.

Connect it. Share how we don't know when Jesus will return, but we know it will happen in the Father's perfect timing.

▼ JESUS CONNECTION ▼

To be ready for Jesus' return doesn't mean we'll have a suitcase packed. It means we'll do what we should be doing while we wait. One of the main things we should do is tell others about Jesus. Our love for Jesus and our love for others is best displayed when we share the gospel. To be ready, then, is to learn how to share about Jesus and to look for times to tell others the gospel—the best news of all.

▶ How can you learn and practice telling others about Jesus?

99. WHAT WILL HAPPEN WHEN JESUS RETURNS?

When Jesus returns, all the dead will be raised to life, unbelievers to eternal judgment and believers to eternal reward.

REVELATION 20:11-15; 21:1-4 (OR 20:12; 21:4)

As believers, we can be excited about Jesus' return! But Jesus' return won't be good news for unbelievers. Unbelievers will be raised from the dead to face judgment for their unforgiven sins. They won't be able to talk their way out of this and it will be too late to repent and trust in Jesus (Hebrews 9:27). Instead, every person who faces this judgment will acknowledge that Jesus is Lord, not for salvation, but to admit they deserve the judgment for sin they're about to receive (Philippians 2:10-11). Then they will face what the Bible calls the "second death," in which they'll be forever separated from God's love and provision.

While this can be difficult for us to think about, there's good news. First, as believers, we won't face this judgment and we won't experience the "second death." Second, as believers we can tell as many people as we can about Jesus so they'll be spared from this coming judgment.

Although unbelievers have good reason to dread Jesus' return, we don't. We can be excited about Jesus' return and eager for it to happen (Hebrews 9:28). The return of Jesus is good news for us! When Jesus returns, we'll be with Jesus and all other believers and be rewarded for our faithfulness.

How amazing is that? Being forgiven of sin and adopted as God's children is reward enough, but God will go beyond that and reward us for doing what we should do anyway—live faithfully for his glory. We don't know what these rewards will be, but whatever they are, they will be the "icing on the cake." Our greatest joy is that we'll finally be with Jesus. We'll see Jesus face to face and be with him and all other believers forevermore.

▶ *What do you think you will first want to do when you see Jesus?*

WHAT WILL HAPPEN WHEN JESUS RETURNS?

▶ How do you feel about seeing Jesus one day?

1 — 2 — 3 — 4 — 5 — 6 — 7 — 8 — 9 — 10
KIND OF NERVOUS   REALLY EXCITED

▶ What questions do you have so far?

▶ What are you wondering about because of what you've heard?

PRAYER

God, thank you for the promise of Jesus' return and that when he does, we'll experience great reward, best of all being with you. Amen.

FAMILY ACTIVITY: PLAY

Do it. Play several rounds of rock-paper-scissors or a quick game like it, providing a small reward (e.g., piece of candy, nickel) each time someone wins a round.

Discuss it. Talk about how it felt to get the rewards so quickly and so often.

Connect it. Share how God has promised us rewards too. While we won't see most of these rewards right away, we can be sure that they'll be far better than the rewards in the game!

▼ JESUS CONNECTION ▼

In the Gospels, Jesus raised a few people from the dead, like Lazarus. These resurrections weren't final; all these people died again. But when Jesus returns, all the dead will be raised permanently. We can't raise anyone from the dead, but we can do something like it. We can tell people about Jesus and pray they trust in him to be forgiven of their sins so they will live with Jesus forever.

▶ Who can you tell about Jesus this week?

Appendix A

LEADING YOUR CHILD TO FAITH IN JESUS

FAMILY DISCIPLESHIP ISN'T ABOUT TEACHING our children the truths and ways of God so they'll behave better. Family discipleship is about teaching our children the truths and ways of God so they'll come to know, love, and trust in Jesus, be forgiven of their sins, be made new in the image of Christ, and then live out their amazing new identity in Christ. Living differently is surely a big part of it, but the way we get to that makes all the difference. And trusting in Jesus is the lynchpin to it all.

Throughout the devotions in *Faith Foundations*, you may notice several references to the Rescuer. That person is, of course, Jesus. The Son of God came to earth two thousand years ago to fulfill the promise made in Genesis 3:15 and be the one who would crush sin and death under his foot and rescue all who believe in him from sin's bondage. That includes your child. If your son or daughter has not yet trusted in Jesus, God shares your heart for that to happen. He longs for your child to come to saving faith. And he has given you a wonderful gift: the calling and privilege to share the gospel with your child. In doing so, we pray that it will lead to his or her profession of faith in Jesus.

Yes, this can be intimidating, but it doesn't need to be. Sharing the gospel isn't as complicated as it might seem. In fact, one of the best ways to share the gospel is to follow the outline of the Bible. Here is a suggested six-part gospel outline with each part's corresponding section of Scripture:

1. **God made us to be his friends**; Act 1: God Creates (Genesis 1–2)
2. **We all have sinned and that sin has broken our friendship with God**; Act 2: People Disobey (Genesis 3–11)
3. **God promised to send a Rescuer**; Act 3: God Promises Jesus (Genesis 12–Malachi 4)

4. **God sent the Rescuer, Jesus, who makes us right with God**; Act 4: God Provides Jesus (Matthew 1–John 20)
5. **We can obey God and live for him because of Jesus**; Act 5: Believers Obey (Acts 1–Revelation 3)
6. **God is sending Jesus back one day**; Act 6: God Re-Creates (Revelation 4–22)

What follows is a suggested way to share the gospel with your child using this outline. The big ideas from it will appear **in bold**. You can simply read what follows, or you can use it to help you develop your own gospel conversation. Whatever you do, remember that God is for you in this important endeavor and he has given you the Holy Spirit to guide you!

Did you know that God made you to be his friend? The Bible begins by telling us that God created everything that exists and he made people most special of all. That includes you! God loves you and he wants you to know him and to love him. Never forget that you're special and that God loves you.

But there's a problem. **We all have sinned and that sin has broken our friendship with God.** In Eden, God told Adam and Eve that there was one thing they couldn't do: eat the fruit from one special tree. Adam and Eve had all they could ever want and need, but they made the terrible decision to disobey God. That's called sin. Sin is anything we want or do that God has forbidden—like eating that fruit. It's also when we don't do what God has told us to do. Everyone disobeys God at times. That's what Romans 3:23 tells us: "For all have sinned and fall short of the glory of God."

Because of sin, our friendship with God has been broken. God still loves us and he still wants to be our friend. That hasn't changed. But our sin is like a barrier that keeps us away from him. God is holy and perfect. We're unholy and imperfect. And those two simply can't mix. It's like oil and water. You can put oil and water together in a jar and shake and shake and shake, but they'll never mix. They'll always separate. And that's what our sins have done between us and God.

So we have a problem we can't fix. But what we broke, God can fix. And that's exactly what he did.

When God disciplined Adam and Eve for their disobedience in Eden, he made an important promise in Genesis 3:15. **God promised to send a Rescuer.** He promised that he would send someone to fix the problem we've made. This Rescuer would make a way—*the* way—for us to be friends with God again. God was talking about Jesus! Jesus would be the perfect Rescuer to fix the problem our sin caused. He would make the one and only way for us to be God's friends again. The rest of the Old Testament shares the story of how God grew the family of a man named Abraham. We know this family as the Israelites. This would be Jesus' family.

Then, in his perfect time, **God sent the Rescuer, Jesus, who makes us right with God.** That's what the first four books of the New Testament—Matthew, Mark, Luke, and John—are about. And that's why they're called Gospels because they tell us the good news, the gospel, about Jesus! Jesus is the Son of God who came to earth and lived a perfect life. He never disobeyed God—not even once. He performed amazing miracles and told people how they could be friends with God. He also explained what it looks like to live the way God made people to live—loving God, worshiping God, serving God, and obeying God.

Although Jesus never did anything wrong, he was arrested and sent to die on a cross. But that was part of God's plan! Jesus died to pay the penalty for our sins. But Jesus didn't stay dead. He rose from the dead on the third day and was seen by his friends called the disciples and many other people. Then, forty days later, Jesus returned to heaven to be with God the Father.

This is good news, but it can get even better than that. When you believe that Jesus is real, that he is the Son of God who died and rose again, and that his death paid the penalty your sins deserve, you will be forgiven of all your sins and become friends with God. That's what Romans 10:9 tells us: "If you confess with your mouth that Jesus is Lord and believe in your heart that God raised him from the dead, you will be saved." This good news becomes the most wonderful, amazing, fantastic, incredible, magnificent news when you trust in Jesus and you are forgiven!

This is all too good to be true, isn't it? But wait! It gets even better! **When you are saved, you can obey God and live for him because of Jesus.**

After Jesus died, rose again, and returned to heaven, he left his followers to continue the mission he began. His followers were to continue telling the world about how to become friends with God and what it's like to live as God's friends. Jesus' disciples told others the gospel and the church grew and grew. This is what the book of Acts and the letters in the New Testament are about. The church wasn't always perfect; even people who have trusted in Jesus, been forgiven, and become friends with God can still sin and struggle to obey God. But the early believers showed they had been changed by God and they loved him, worshiped him, served him, and obeyed him in ways they couldn't before.

The same is true of you. When you trust in Jesus, you become a new person. God changes you on the inside. He changes your mind and your heart. This is what 2 Corinthians 5:17 tells us: "So then, if anyone is in Christ, he is a new creation; what is old has passed away—look, what is new has come!"

You will still struggle to obey God at times—we all do—but you will find that God continues to help you grow and live more like Jesus. And when you do that, you will experience the joy and purpose in life God meant you to have. And you will also be able to help others come to know Jesus and trust in him too.

There's one more important, amazing part of Jesus' rescue. **God is sending Jesus back one day.** That's what the last book of the Bible, Revelation, is about. Revelation tells us how Jesus will return to earth one day and make all things right again. Jesus will make everything not just as good as it was in Eden back in Genesis, but he will make everything even better.

God gave Revelation to us because he wants us to have hope—a confident expectation—that all that sin has broken will be fixed again. The world around us isn't what it should be in so many ways. And even we struggle to obey God. It's difficult and frustrating! We still are sad at times, get sick, and are wronged by others. None of that is how God made things to be. But we know that Jesus is coming back again—it could be at any time—and when he does, all those difficult things will be over. We will spend forever with Jesus and all others who have trusted in him, loving God, worshiping God, serving God, and obeying God perfectly as we were meant to.

Does this all make sense to you?

Do you believe it?

Would you like to trust in Jesus right now?

If so, all you need to do is pray. Prayer is simply talking with God. And in this prayer, you can just talk with God and tell him you believe that Jesus is who the Bible says he is and that Jesus lived a perfect life, died, and rose from the dead. And that on the cross, Jesus paid the punishment you deserve for your sins. You can also tell God that you accept his gift of forgiveness given to you because of Jesus.

Would you like to do that?

Appendix B

TIPS FOR MEMORIZING THE FAMILY CATECHISM

MEMORIZING GOD'S WORD IS a wonderful way to get it into your mind more deeply, and when that happens, it's more likely it will get into your heart too. When that happens, it can be a game-changer for following Jesus! The more your heart loves Jesus, the more your life will show it. The same is true when it comes to memorizing truths about God, like the ones you'll cover in The Family Catechism. As you walk through the family devotions in *Faith Foundations*, one of the best ways you can extend what you learn is to memorize the catechism questions and answers as a family. Here are a few tips to help you do that.

SHARE WHY YOU ARE MEMORIZING

Some kids find memorizing fun. If that's true in your home, then you're good to go! But for other kids who might struggle with memorizing, or who might even resist it and see it as a chore, you'll want to do your best to explain why memorization matters. Remind them often how what you're memorizing is for their good. God's truths aren't just facts to know, they're the key to loving God and enjoying life to the fullest, the way God designed it!

MEMORIZE TOGETHER

Lead by example! When you memorize The Family Catechism, you help prove why it matters. Beyond that, doing things together is always better and more enjoyable. So dive in there and memorize God's truths too!

ENCOURAGE, CHALLENGE, AND REWARD

A mixture of encouraging, challenging, and rewarding will be most effective to fuel memorization, but what that ratio is and when each is needed can change. Of these three, be most generous with your encouragement. Offer sincere, specific encouragement as often as possible. That doesn't mean there isn't a place for challenging your child too. Perhaps you can challenge your child to work on memorization for so many minutes a day or to get a part of a question and answer memorized before you can. That leads to rewards. Consider providing modest rewards for completing memorization or at least for attempting memorization. You might also want to offer larger rewards for memorizing larger portions of The Family Catechism.

TALK ABOUT WHAT YOU ARE MEMORIZING

Memorization fuels understanding and understanding fuels memorization. That's why it's important not to stop talking about the question and answer once the family devotion ends. As you work on memorizing a question and answer, look for opportunities to talk more about what it means and how you can live it out. When your child understands what is being memorized, it will be easier to memorize it.

GIVE YOUR KIDS MEMORIZATION "TOOLS"

Beyond the tips provided above, there are a bunch of "tools" to help foster memorization. Think of these as tools in a tool belt that can be used as needed. Some might be used all the time, others rarely, if ever. And that's okay. Find the tools that work best and use them as you need them.

Concentrate. This is becoming increasingly difficult in our culture. Distractions are all around us, and most often it's right there in our hands in the form of a phone or device. When it comes time to work on memorization, remove or reduce as many distractions as possible.

"Chunk" the content. Break up longer content into chunks. Then work on memorizing a chunk at a time and put those memorized chunks together.

Focus on key words. At least at first, focus on key words—those that are most essential to convey the idea of what's being memorized. Then fill in the smaller words around them, with these key words often being the trigger to help in that process.

Build and link the content. When memorizing something new, it's often helpful to link it to something you already know. The order of

The Family Catechism often does this for you. Be sure to make these connections clear.

Repeat the content. Repeating the content verbally is one of the most familiar and effective memorization techniques. This includes reviewing what has been already memorized to keep it fresh. The adage rings true: use it or lose it.

Write the content. An effective complement to repeating content aloud is writing it. We engage a different part of our brains when we write.

Use flash cards. One place to write the content is on flash cards. Write the question on one side and the answer on the other. Then use these cards when your family is memorizing content or when someone wants to do some extra work on his or her own. Think of "down times" when flash cards can be handy to use, such as while brushing teeth in the morning and evening.

Sing the content. Put the content to a song you know, or create a song just for it. It's not surprising that music greatly aids in memorization. The odds are that you know far more song lyrics than anything else.

Draw the content. This is especially helpful for visual learners. Draw a picture or pictures that represent the question and answer. The act of thinking about what to draw and then drawing it goes a long way in memorization, and then reviewing the drawing helps even more.

Review before sleeping. What's on your mind right before going to sleep often sticks with you. Partner this tip with the others and have the flash cards or drawings handy by the bed, reviewing the content together right before bed.

Incorporate exercise. Not only is exercise good for us, it also helps memorizing. Consider times when walking, jogging, biking, or playing can be integrated into memorizing content.

Appendix C

WAYS TO PRAY AS A FAMILY

PRAYER IS SIMPLY TALKING WITH GOD (see The Family Catechism question eighty-five), but even so, many people find it challenging to pray by themselves, let alone with others. Often, part of the problem is that we simply don't know where to begin or what to say. It's one thing to talk with someone we can see and hear talking back; it's another thing to talk with God—we know he's there, but we cannot see him or hear him audibly.

With that in mind, below are several prayer techniques you can use as part of the devotions in this book, at bedtime, before meals, on the way to school, or any other time you pray. Find one or two to use regularly or mix them up. The choice is yours. Regardless of the technique or techniques you use, consider keeping a family prayer journal to record requests, celebrations, answered prayers, and other highlights from your family prayer times.

THE ACTS METHOD

This popular technique uses an acronym to separate your time of prayer into four parts. A is for *adoration*, when you begin by sharing reasons you are grateful to God for who he is. C is for *confession*, when you share any sins you've committed. You can share these aloud, being careful to be appropriately vulnerable, or you can do this silently or in writing. T is for *thanksgiving*, when you thank God for what he has done recently. Finally, S is for *supplication*, when you share your needs and requests with God.

If you use this method, you can share responses to all four parts and then pray for them all together at the end, pray for each part one at a time, or consider the answers everyone shares as the prayer itself.

THE BREATHE METHOD

In this technique, you pray literally as you breathe. On the inhale, focus on receiving something from God—a promise, part of God's character, an accepted truth, and so forth. For example, you might say, "God, I receive your peace," and then inhale. On the exhale, focus on what you need to let go of or trust in God for. So, for example, you might continue by saying, "I let go of my fear about that test tomorrow" and then exhale. Or, on an inhale, you might say something like, "God, I believe that you love me and accept me no matter what." Then on the exhale you might say, "Please help me not compare myself to others."

"ONE THING" PRAYERS

This technique is built on asking a "one thing" question as a prayer prompt. For example, you could ask, "What's one thing you're thankful to God for?" Or, "What's one thing you would like to ask God for?" Or, "Who's one friend you want to pray for?" This technique is especially helpful if time is short or someone seems distracted or disengaged. The prayer could even simply be the answers given.

POPCORN PRAYERS

In this technique, instead of asking one person to pray or taking turns praying, a more "organic" approach is taken. Begin by providing a prayer prompt—this could even be used with another technique like the ACTS method. Then let people say a word, phrase, or sentence prayer in response to that prompt. For example, if the prompt was, "What do you love most about God?" some popcorn prayers could be, "He is faithful," "He loves me," "He has forgiven me," and so forth. One word of encouragement is needed for this technique: be comfortable with moments of silence! Wait them out. Give your family time to think and respond.

SENTENCE PRAYERS

This technique is similar to popcorn praying, but it asks for each person to simply give a one-sentence prayer. These prayers could be according to a prompt, or they can be whatever each person wants to say to God.

PRAYING SCRIPTURE

For this technique, choose passages of Scripture that include promises from God, commands from God, or descriptions of God. The Psalms are often great to use. Other types of passages would also work, but they might be more challenging. Then read a line of Scripture and pray in response to it. It could be thanking God, or asking for strength and guidance to obey God, or whatever else the Holy Spirit prompts based on the Scripture you just read.

RESPONSIVE PRAYER

This technique focuses on listening to the Holy Spirit rather than on what we might want to say to God. Put on some worship music, instrumental music, an audio Bible, or even a sound machine. Choose a length of time and strive not to say anything. Rather, seek to still your heart and mind and listen to the Holy Spirit.

RHYTHMIC PRAYER

This technique can be especially meaningful for those who struggle to sit still. Begin by softly patting your lap and clapping your hands to develop a rhythm. Once the rhythm is established, take turns saying a prayer in sync with the rhythm.

NOTES

HOW TO USE FAITH FOUNDATIONS

[1] "Leaning Tower of Pisa," *Britannica*, accessed February 24, 2025, www.britannica.com/topic/Leaning-Tower-of-Pisa; and "Leaning Tower of Pisa Facts," Leaning Tower of Pisa, accessed February 24, 2025, www.towerofpisa.org/leaning-tower-of-pisa-facts.

[2] *Catechism* comes from the Greek word *katēcheō*, which means to "teach by word of mouth" or "instruct" (Henry George Liddell, Robert Scott, et al., *A Greek-English Lexicon* [Oxford, UK: Clarendon, 1996], 927). This word is used seven times in the New Testament, notably of Apollos's instruction (Acts 18:25), Paul's desire to instruct others (1 Corinthians 14:19), and Paul's command that those who receive instruction in the Word must share good things with those who teach it (Galatians 6:6). The other four occurrences are Luke 1:4; Acts 21:21, 24; and Romans 2:18.

[3] Here are a few related terms: *catechesis* (the form of instruction), *catechism* (the content of instruction), *catechumen* (the recipient of instruction), *catechist* (the giver of instruction), and *catechize* (the process of instruction).

10. WHAT DOES IT MEAN THAT GOD IS OMNISCIENT?

[1] "2023 Major League Baseball Pitching Pitches," Baseball Reference, 2023, www.baseball-reference.com/leagues/majors/2023-pitches-pitching.shtml.

[2] "Number of Hairs on Human Head," BioNumbers, accessed November 28, 2024, https://bionumbers.hms.harvard.edu/bionumber.aspx?id=101509.